ALWAYS IN
THE DARK

ALWAYS IN THE DARK

ONE WOMAN'S SEARCH FOR ANSWERS FROM A FAMILY SHROUDED IN SECRETS

DIANE HARDING

www.blkdogpublishing.com

For my mother for remaining by my side

PROLOGUE

I woke up to discover my long-time ambition staring me in the face. It was 2006 and news that my stepmother had died sent me rushing for my laptop to begin typing events I could recall from my youth. With her death, the last of those involved, finally, I had my guilt-free ticket to chart the extraordinary years. I had waited an eternity for this opportunity, and it would not be a day too soon to put the record straight.

As a little girl, I would sometimes joke with my mother that I would one day write a book. She'd laugh, tell me it was a splendid idea and ask if she would feature. Her death in 2003 had provided me with startling information I had not known existed. It seemed she had remembered the threat I made as a child. Stashed away in a battered Fairy Liquid box was a carefully written note on top of her confidential papers written in heavy black ink. **DIANE. FOR YOUR BOOK ONE DAY?** Untouched for years it emerged that my mother's secret box had followed her around the country accumulating evidence.

Diane Harding

Blanche in 1948

CHAPTER 1
THE CALL

I banged my mobile down on the black granite breakfast bar.
'Bitch!' I screamed.

It was a hot July morning in 2006. Connie was in a coma. But a coma? I had heard of people regaining consciousness. That meant I was still in with a chance. I tried to pull myself together knowing that she and I had crucial unfinished business.

Connie had been my stepmother for the last thirty-two years, having married my ambitious and dictatorial father, Victor, within weeks of my parents' acrimonious divorce. That was in 1974, when I was twenty-five. Frivolous and self-assured Connie was the opposite in every way to my petite, demure and long-suffering mother, Blanche.

I have never ceased to wonder what made Connie behave the way she did. Why did she do it? What possessed her? I have asked myself a thousand times. She was a likeable character who drew people into her world with an infectious smile and bubbly personality.

'And did she say anything? Anything at all?' I asked the hospital nurse. I needed to know.

'Well, soon after being admitted, Connie told me she'd lived in Cape Town.'

I waited. 'And?'

'And that you're her stepdaughter.'

'Anything else?'

3

'Only that she lived over there for a long time … with a family. That's all.'

'If she rallies round, just tell her I'm waiting. She'll understand.' I spelt out every syllable in a loud voice. I was hoping Connie might clear her conscience before departing this world.

I could not contain myself so the following morning I telephoned the hospital.

'She's peaceful,' the nurse told me in a Liverpudlian accent. 'There's no change I'm afraid.' She sounded apologetic. 'I really think you ought to visit again before it's too late. Judy's at her bedside.'

I remembered Judy, with her warm smile and unflappable nature. Living opposite my stepmother in Southport, she was the daughter of Connie's close friend, Freda, from way back when they had both won school scholarships. I envisioned Judy's gentle manner as she cradled Connie's hand with her soothing tones offering comfort.

'Who's that on the phone?' my husband, Chris, shouted from the bottom of the garden.

'Hospital telling me I should go back up,' I yelled through the open kitchen window. 'She's just the same.'

Although gripped by a sense of urgency that she may not be around much longer, I told the nurse I would not be hurtling back up to Southport as I was there the previous weekend and it was a four-hundred-mile round trip.

'For goodness sake.' Chris wandered back towards the house; his shirt covered in mahogany splodges from his fence staining task. 'I was hoping you'd come to your senses.'

'Okay, Okay. No need to go through that again.' I felt myself prickle at his reaction. 'I've lost count how many times I've made the journey. I've been a *brick*!'

'You have. And I know Connie's always insisted you don't travel all that way, but she's been worried sick, poor woman. I realize she isn't a blood relative, but she did marry your father.'

'She's going to die, I know it.'

'Of course. That's what usually follows a coma.' He seemed puzzled, but I had unearthed a wealth of startling evidence I had not told him about.

Chris was right. She was independent, with never any expectation of a visit. 'You don't get a minute, working full time at that school,' she would say. But whenever we visited, her crushing hugs were dependable. The affection between us had been mutual in those early days but, because she was adamant for me not to make the journey towards the end, part of me wondered whether she could not bring herself to admit to any wrongdoing. Or was it because she did not want me to see how she had deteriorated; no longer able to keep those irresistible looks for which she had been renowned?

Chris's grilling continued, unable to let the matter rest.

'I'd have driven you back up. You know I would.'

That was the moment I realized how fortunate I was to have someone so considerate for a husband. Although he had a pressurised position in the Ministry of Defence, once home, he was tolerant and easy-going even if it meant foregoing his insatiable thirst for golf. Always ready to fall in step with my arrangements; this was one of the reasons, I guess, our marriage has stood the course of time.

'I know you're frustrated,' I said, kicking at the gravel chippings in the barbecue courtyard, 'but my mind's made up. I wonder how many people refuse to dash to the dying?'

'Don't know, but you're one of them.'

And did I feel guilty that I had refused to see Connie? Not in the least.

'You don't understand,' I told him.

'I don't. Not sure what's come over you. In all our married years, I've never seen you acting this way.'

'That's enough. Do NOT keep on!' I felt I would snap if he said anything more. I had not been sleeping well, and things were beginning to take their toll. I knew I was under scrutiny, but I had only myself to blame; I had no intention of letting him know what I was going through. The whole scenario of my background was an embarrassing one and, for now, best kept secret.

'Better ring the kids.

'I *will*. When the time's right.'

Chris rolled his eyes. 'They need to know.'

'For God's sake. They're young adults now. I'll ring them when they've finished work.'

'Not her real grandchildren, I know. But as good as. You

have to remember that.'

How could I forget. It was obvious my home life was a weird one and my discovery of this not until adulthood was beyond baffling. But I was a young child when it all began. Compared to my friends, my life appeared a mystery and it's only now, looking back, I wonder why I was so surprised when I unearthed the evidence. I can't believe I didn't see it. Everything was there in front of my eyes but, over the years, it seems I had taken the situation for granted and had lived my life to the point of naivety.

Shrewd and educated, Connie had a great deal to answer for. As I studied her propped up on crisp lily-white pillows in her hospital bed the previous Saturday it defied belief to think she had been the cause of so much upheaval in my home.

I felt Chris's comforting arm round my shoulder. 'Let it out,' he said. 'Do you good … you know, cathartic.'

With that, salty tears stung my eyes. But these were tears of a different kind, not for someone I'd once known and was about to lose, but for my past that had come scuttling back.

I was thankful I had been able to push the unfair events to the back of my mind, determined never to allow them to haunt me. I imagined that what I had lived through had taught me to be strong and to cope but now decades-old incidents had attacked my thinking and felt as though they had happened yesterday. I was surprised just how much I could recall from my youth as strong memories of growing up in the Cape during the Fifties and Sixties jostled for my attention.

What my own children and, more importantly, Chris, who I had married in 1971, did not appreciate was that I had become encased in a shell of secrecy that was impossible to crack. Even more staggering, I had been sitting on the evidence for the past three years since my mother's death. Although I had never talked about my past, I'd negotiated with myself, deciding silence was my best option. Because of the stigma it carried, it was out of the question to tell anyone.

It had become a dilemma. Only two days earlier, Chris and I had sauntered along romantic country lanes and through fields of unkempt cow parsley to reach the clump of trees at the top of Kelston Hill. We rested on a bench to catch our breath, so I'd had every opportunity. We kept no secrets from one another, but remaining silent was how I had learnt to deal with my life. I hadn't even let slip that I was writing about my background, as that would mean opening a deep chasm. I felt guilty. I trusted Chris and wondered whether it was right to treat him in this way but knew the least said the better, although I was beginning to wish I had told him the truth long before now.

I had no idea how I would ever be able to let go of my shameful secret. I needed to free myself from the burden that had blighted me for so long, but I also knew that the longer I avoided the subject, the harder it would be to let go. The compassion in Chris's voice told me he was aware there had been tricky times between my parents and that I'd surfaced from troubled waters, but that was only half the story and, for now, that was all he was going to know.

I promised myself that one day I would unveil the truth.

But for now, *now* was not the time.

Diane Harding

CHAPTER 2
SOUTH AFRICA BECKONS

'My dear Vicky met me with a huge bunch of flowers. I was thrilled to see him again. We may have a baby.'

Those were the words my mother had written in her diary after she set foot on Cape Town soil. After a four-month separation, finally she had joined her Vicky who had set sail for South Africa in 1948, three years after the Second World War had ended. Born in 1918, they had met as teenagers, introduced to one another by a mutual friend, and although his wartime duties had taken him away, their relationship continued to flourish.

With my mother's slender and graceful features and my father's strong chiselled jawline they were a glamorous couple and in 1940 married at St Francis Xavier Catholic Church in Hereford, the same church where my father donned white robes and practised as an altar boy during his adolescent years. The one wedding vow my mother agreed to abide by was to raise any offspring in the Catholic faith, a commitment that would cause problems.

Blanche and Victor in 1936 when they first met

Blanche and Victor's Wedding Day, March 1940

With England in the grip of post-war poverty and cities and towns in crumbled ruin, a £200 incentive for ex-servicemen to build a property had my ambitious father hooked on the idea of emigrating. And with encouraging reports from his younger sister, Nancy, and husband, Stan, who had settled in South Africa the previous year, followed soon after by their youngest brother, Billy, his yearning intensified. Everything would be paradise compared to the squalor and hardship endured during the war.

For my timid mother to sail off into the unknown was a courageous undertaking but all fears of travelling alone evaporated when my father told her how he was confident they had made the right decision and how he was impatient for her to join him to share in the sophisticated lifestyle.

In her diary, she wrote:

'The Mediterranean became rough and was not blue. People looked sickly and disappeared from dining rooms. I took some Kwells and wasn't sick, although boat rolling horribly. Sat wrapped up on deck and my steward brought lunch up to me. Our fourth berth now occupied by a foreigner, Greek!! Arrived Port Said. Wonderful sight. Officials came on board and boats alongside selling their wares. Natives loading oil. Noisy. Rose early next morning to see Suez Canal. Interesting to see the camels. Very little breeze. Weather becoming hot and sticky and difficult to sleep at night. Crew now wearing their white uniforms and passengers starting to look sunburnt. Crossed the equator and one perspires freely below deck. Wore long dress to have champagne and savouries with captain. Checked in through customs at Durban to catch train. Passed through miles of barren country growing corn and cactus. Surrounded by mountains and wasteland. Caught Johannesburg Express train and arrived Cape Town.'

For the initial few months, a hotel was home for my parents; my mother relieved her boredom with dressmaking and helping at the Estate Agency offices, a business partnership my father had entered into, but within months he had accepted a permanent position with Cadbury's, a role overseeing the offices and storage depot in the centre of Cape Town.

Nine months later, I made my entrance at Leighwood Maternity Home. I was my father's thirtieth birthday gift, there was no denying that and, from what I gather, was lucky to be born a girl as he had made it clear he did not relish the idea of a son, the reason to this day a mystery.

The normal hectic times with a baby took their course and with my father's 'only-the-best-will-do' attitude, ten weeks later, on a sunny Palm Sunday my christening took place at St George's Cathedral in Cape Town.

Diane's Christening, April 1949

Washington Road in Claremont, a suburb populated by white middle-class inhabitants was where I spent the first ten years of my life. Colour-washed a subtle shade of pomegranate it was a property my parents were proud of and, given my father's passion for gardening, our vibrant zinnia borders were a show stopper and our gardenia bush with its intoxicating aroma wafting from delicate cream flowers in the evening warmth always a talking point for passers-by.

Blanche with Diane, aged nine months

We had all the latest mod cons including a telephone on the wall in the hall, a rarity back in those days. The bungalow offered three bedrooms; one for my parents, one for me and the third for guests when we were lucky enough to have visitors from England.

My parents' arrival in South Africa in 1948 coincided with the introduction of apartheid which gave white people ascendancy over everything. Stringent rules made mixed marriages illegal, with non-whites discriminated against in public areas and on transport. I remember black South Africans sitting in their designated seating with signs 'Moenie spu nie' – do not spit. My parents found it difficult adjusting to the harsh regime and felt uneasy having to abide by the visible horrors of the system. As outsiders, it was an eye opener. My mother said it didn't seem right that, because you were born one colour, the law dictated segregation from those of others, unable to comprehend why the government imposed the barbaric legislation. The injustice of it made her feel uncomfortable and humbled but, born into the system, I was unaware of its existence and as I grew up it became a way of life that I accepted with no questions asked.

As most families did, my parents fell in step and employed a servant. Although strict laws dictated that the sleeping quarters were in a separate building away from the main property, they made a conscious decision that they would treat Lydia, our first maid, as part of the family. It was normal for home-helps to be female, either black or Cape coloured, a term used to describe the resultant offspring from mixed races.

Lydia was black and came into my life when I was a baby. As a young child there is one instance that springs to mind when my parents had left me in her charge. Violent storms were common, and the rumbling claps of thunder had woken me. I kept calling but when no-one appeared decided to investigate; the radio was blaring but the house was empty and eerie. I reached for the front door handle and breathed in the smell of fresh rain on parched pavements. Vivid lightening scudded across an angry sky and within seconds giant raindrops had soaked through my thin poplin nightdress. I saw a deserted street except for our curious next-door neighbour, Mr Clinton, who was trying to start his car. He informed me he had seen Lydia haring up the road to her friend. That incident had a profound effect on me; once put to bed it became the norm to call out 'good night'; once I heard a response, I knew it was safe to shut my eyes. Lydia had her marching orders after that event.

Diane with Lydia in the garden in Claremont

Sixteen-year-old Annie of mixed race was her replacement. With a slim figure and white overall nipped in at the waist with a wide black elasticised belt and a white starched cap perched on top of her tight black curls which she held in place with grips, I'd sometimes chase her to knock it off, after which we would dissolve into giggles. We had fun, Annie and I, and with her quiet and coy nature, she assisted my mother with the day-to-day chores around the home.

CHAPTER 3
HOMESICK

Although my mother had adapted well to life abroad, in 1952, four years after her arrival, severe bouts of homesickness began to preoccupy her thoughts. She fantasised about visiting her mother, Fanny, and rekindling the joy of the simple country pleasures she had grown up with. Sunday walks in the apple orchards around Hereford was what she missed most and with every airmail that fell through the letter box, her aching nostalgia intensified.

There was another good reason to visit England; I was heading towards my third birthday and it was time to meet my relatives.

The day my father returned home from work and announced that he had booked our passage, my mother leapt into his arms knowing her long awaited dream had become reality and, because there would be icy temperatures when we arrived in the February, and not the scorching summer heat I was accustomed to, I was kitted out with suitable clothing courtesy of Stuttafords, the finest departmental store in Cape Town.

Eight weeks later, with my name added to my mother's passport, we were ready to embark on the *Pendennis Castle*, one of a fleet of Union Castle ships that transported mail weekly from Southampton to Cape Town. I remember the tall red funnels with thick black smoke belching into a cloudless sky and small tugs that nudged our colossal ship from its berth. I waved my father goodbye; for a tiny child, it was the start of a momentous voyage.

Memories of that journey are hazy, but I recall with vivid accuracy the early morning tea and Nice biscuits brought to our cabin by our white uniformed steward and my early meal times taken in the cavernous dining room before being put to bed so the adults could dress in their finery and enjoy theirs at leisure. I also remember peering through the round porthole in our confined cabin, spellbound by the rise and fall of the dark ocean on the distant horizon and as a special treat being allowed to clamber up the stepladder onto the top bunk.

Diane and Blanche on the Pendennis Castle bound for England, 1952

With a long red scarf and mitts and my new navy coat buttoned under my chin, the morning we disembarked at Southampton I watched as the flag flapped high on the ship's mast in a vicious gale. I clung on to my mother's coat as my legs negotiated the wobbly wooden gangplank and, before I knew it, the wheels on the steam train were clickety clacking towards Waterloo Station in London where, after a journey that appeared endless, my mother's elder sister, Freda, and husband, Frank, were there to meet us under the tall Clock Tower. My uncle Frank was a lean man with a booming voice and had a pipe which he seldom removed clenched between his front teeth.

My mother told me how proud she was introducing me to everyone for the first time and how well I talked for my age, but I felt lost in those new surroundings with people I didn't know. I also discovered new rules I needed to obey.

Blanche and Diane in England with Linda, Freda and Fanny

We shared our time between Grandma's home in Hereford and Freda and Frank's in Surrey, with their two children, David and Peter. Their red brick house adjoined St Lawrence's Primary

School in Effingham, where my uncle was headmaster. I became wary of his stern ways; he ruled with a rod of iron and suffered no nonsense. For me, visions of sitting at the dinner table conjure fear; grace prefixed mealtimes and when I disobeyed orders to shut my eyes, I incurred a sharp rap on the knuckles. I struggled with the strict regime; we never said grace in our home, although my father made sure I observed his standards and, whatever I did, I was never to eat with my mouth open.

This was not the only reprimand that came my way. The toy cupboard my cousins shared on the upstairs landing was a sacred place and I was intrigued. One afternoon, when all was quiet, I took it upon myself to do a little reorganisation and emptied out the entire contents; but I discovered I had been a naughty girl with another severe warning on my uncle's return from school. After that episode, I made sure I kept out of his way.

My mother wrote to my father telling him they had been talking non-stop since arriving. 'So much to catch up on,' she said and, sparing a fretful thought for him without her around, she continued, 'I hope Annie's keeping you supplied with clean shirts!'

Apart from a tartan kilt made for me by Grandma's friend, Mrs Scriven, and pinching my nose to ward off the revolting stench of boiling fish for Auntie Freda's two enormous cats, Shakespeare and Chaucer, my time in England is sketchy but lodged in my mind are strong memories of seeing snow for the first time, the ginger cake Grandma baked me for my third birthday and the telegram I received from my father, sending me his love.

With our stay at an end, I leapt for joy when I learnt that Grandma would be accompanying us back to Cape Town for a holiday of her own. It was one goodbye I would not have to make.

As the *Stirling Castle* cut its course through six thousand miles of calm indigo ocean, Grandma spent much of her time up on deck in search of the cooling breeze and letter writing. And in one of these to Linda, her younger daughter, she wrote:

> 'We have now reached Cape Verde. The steward said it would be hot for two days and then get cooler, but it is too hot for me to do anything. We are near the equator now and I'm slowly frying.'

And then:

> 'We have passed the line and they had the customary ceremony with Father Neptune. I went on the first-class deck and he came up the stairs from the sea! They marched to the bathing pool and it was most amusing to watch the girls and children ducked and then get buckets of water thrown over them. The whole thing terrified Diane in case it involved her.'

Finally, she told her:

> 'Diane is now saying that she will soon see her daddy. Will have more news after we land. Your loving Mother xx'

It was the return journey from England that I remember more than anything; twelve weeks had been an eternity to be away from my father and the thought of him hugging me became more important than anything.

As that warm comforting sun appeared on the horizon, the minute we docked I watched hefty ropes secure our ship to gigantic concrete bollards and covered my ears as deafening cranes whirred into action. Impatient to spot him amongst the heaving crowds below, I craned my head through the white railings and waved my hand into space. From high up everyone on the ground appeared minute but then I picked him out, my shrieks of joy impossible to control as I tried to keep track of him.

'Daddy, Daddy!' I screamed as he threw Cadbury's chocolate bars up on to the scrubbed wooden deck with amazing accuracy. But his final attempt landed under a nun's deckchair. An enormous black cross dangled round her neck and caught my attention. She appeared amused by his antics and beckoned for me to retrieve his offering.

With strict instructions from my mother not to mention the tomato seeds hidden in my little handbag, she whispered them to me one last time as we entered the gigantic customs shed. Forbidden to bring them into the country, these were the words she had drummed in me for days. Once through immigration, both of us sprinted the last few yards and with her bubbly smile, tears welled as my father lowered a bouquet of perfumed red roses into her arms.

'I've missed you,' I told him as he whisked me into the air. But the moment was too much. 'Guess what I've got for you?' my whisper loud enough for all to hear.

'Shhh!' My mother pressed her finger to my lips.

I was back with my wonderful father, and Grandma was with us too. What more could I ask?

Packed to the gunwhales with our luggage and souvenirs, our sandy coloured Dodge travelled along De Waal Drive en route for home. I sat next to Grandma in the back of a stifling car and watched intrigued as she fanned herself with the hem of her long black skirt. We all laughed at the sight of it, Grandma too seeing the funny side of her flapping performance. She also had a small bottle of something called smelling salts which she inhaled along the journey. As a three-year-old, I could not understand the need, because I was not aware that salt smelt of anything.

Separated from my father for so long, I was anxious to off-fload my news. I needed to tell him about my escapades and adventures; how the best thing about my holiday was the frozen white flakes that fell out of the sky and the worst the disgusting smell of boiling fish for Shakespeare and Chaucer's dinner. I also told him how my uncle Frank had walloped me and that I had a new kilt with a huge pin in it. So much had happened.

Although he did not appear to be joining in the fun, my mother gabbled away as she pointed out the places of interest to Grandma; Lion's Head and Cape Town University on the right with Cecil Rhodes Memorial in the foreground. She seemed delighted to have seen the enormous statue with her own eyes, while the zebra, grazing idly on the craggy slopes of Table Mountain, made her squeal.

The next few miles were a blur. All I recall is the mention of a visitor. I pricked up my ears. We already had my grandma coming to stay so who could this be? Being an only child, the prospect of someone I could involve in my make-believe world had me bouncing in my seat.

As the conversation continued, I heard the name Connie.

CHAPTER 4
A VISITOR ARRIVES

I t seemed I was going to have not one but two playmates. It did not get any better than that. Inquisitive, and at the same time impatient, I couldn't wait to meet our guest. Would she have a nice face? Would she be friendly? Would she speak to me? So many thoughts crammed my mind.

After the announcement that we had a visitor, no-one spoke for the remainder of the journey until we pulled up in the drive and my father broadcast in a loud voice, 'Home at last.' He tooted the horn and a tanned young lady with an enormous smile emerged onto the veranda. 'This is Connie, sweetheart,' he said.

I rushed over and sniffed her delicious perfume. 'I've heard all about you,' she whispered as she bent down to my level. My mother did not acknowledge her but barged past and stomped to her bedroom. I could not understand why she did not say hello because I thought it was polite to greet someone if you had not met them before.

The appearance of our guests contrasted one another. With earthy brown eyes and bouncy brunette curls Connie had a mischievous glint. She sported knee-length dirndl skirts and tight tops that exaggerated her pointy breasts, whereas Grandma displayed a seriousness, wore skirts down to her ankles and frilly blouses that covered her arms. But it was the gold-rimmed cameo brooch pinned on the front of her lapel that caught my eye as did her lace-up shoes and thick brown stockings that rippled at the ankles.

With all those garments, it was small wonder she complained of the heat.

With the arrival of our visitors, the exploration of beaches took priority; a wealth of coastlines offered hidden coves and rocky escarpments while others had an uninterrupted expanse of smooth ivory sand. The thrill of those outings was as though it was my first and when my father shouted, 'I'm first to see the sea!' I'd wind down the car window and breathe in the faint taste of salt. Although spoilt for choice, we had our favourites; the pearly sands and sophistication of Clifton beach, or Dalebrook, a hidden gem with its safe bathing in the shallow tidal pool close to Simon's Town, then a Naval base. They all had their own charm, but my father's preference was Gordon's Bay, a thirty-mile journey along an endless parched and dusty road where windmills worked overtime in the stifling breeze. With his car down on its axles and two hessian water carriers anchored to the front bumper, tea making courtesy of the primus stove took priority the minute we arrived.

Connie, Diane and Blanche at the beach

With my body doused in olive oil, I'd rush down to the shoreline, wading into the waves until they slammed against my body. 'Be careful now,' my mother would shout. 'Not too far.' She

24

had never learnt to swim, so danger hovered at the forefront of her mind. Sizzling under a sweltering heat, the glinting sea lapped at our toes and lofty palm trees offered shade to nut brown sun worshippers. Shell collecting and the building of sandcastles were an important part of the day together with the obligatory exploration of rock pools still wet and slippery from the receding tide.

But the euphoria of these visits came with a minor drawback; the lack of public toilets. When it was time to spend a penny, my mother escorted me down to a rocky ridge of prickly gorse bushes behind a tiny but perfectly formed white-washed church. If it was a Sunday, melodic and tuneful singing from the black congregation filled the air, the sound of that sweet-sounding harmony I will always hold dear.

On our homeward journey, with roads a shimmering inferno and my head nodding from exhaustion, he always made the perfect end to a fun day by pulling in at the roadside to buy an armful of mealies (corn on the cob) from enthusiastic black traders eager to clinch a deal. Freshly cut from the fields, the aroma when they boiled in the pot made my mouth water, and if I were lucky, he would bundle a gigantic watermelon into the boot.

What was to have been a thrilling holiday for my grandma appeared over-shadowed by the presence of Auntie Connie and as a dutiful mother-in-law she wasted no time in lecturing my father that he should have consulted my mother before her arrival. Fanny's thoughts were with her daughter and she hoped he would see the misery he was inflicting. But he ignored her advice. No-one was going to tell him what to do and from that day his relationship with his mother-in-law soured, his dislike of her poking her nose into his affairs following him to the grave.

Connie despised domesticity. I never saw her with her hands in the washing-up water but instead, clad in skimpy shorts and a bikini top, she preferred to sunbathe in our back-garden amongst the lemon, plum and kumquat trees. Sprawled out sipping her favourite tipple of chilled Castle beer, she indulged in Black Magic chocolates taken from a glossy black box with a red ribbon and tassel which she kept hidden in the kitchen cupboard out of my father's sight; only Cadbury's chocolate was good enough.

Connie sunbathing

After four months in Cape Town, Grandma's holiday ended but with no sign of our other guest leaving my mother must have felt deep resentment and at times, I presume, an attitude that was polite but distant. Some might have said she was over tolerant but all these years later I could understand why.

Like all young children, I wallowed in my parents' attention until one day I heard an argument. Because I had not witnessed them quarrel before, it sent me rushing to my bedroom in tears. I pulled my silky pink eiderdown over my ears and hoped I would never hear raised voices again but there were further disagreements and I couldn't understand why times had gone from cheery and carefree to sometimes troublesome and tricky.

I asked my mother why this was, but she never gave an answer.

CHAPTER 5
THE INQUISITION BEGINS

It was July 2006 and time to contact Linda. It was a while since I had seen my eighty-three-year-old energetic aunt, my mother's younger sister by six years. It would be a perfect opportunity to visit her again. Knowing how my mother always felt at ease confiding in her rather than with her older sister, Freda, now in her nineties and with a memory not as alert, she was the one person I knew I could count on. Because I needed to piece together a complicated jigsaw, I hoped she would be able to furnish me with the vital missing links from my parents' past. She was my only hope.

I dialled her Cheltenham number.

'Linda!' I felt relieved she was in. I explained my urgency to talk and agreed that I would see her the following Friday.

Chris often accompanied me but because he was still clueless about my family's history, I opted for a day when I knew he would be playing golf.

I decided not to travel on the motorway but would take the scenic route through Nailsworth, a honey-gold Cotswold village, in the hope the ninety-minute journey would relax me for what I anticipated might be an emotional morning.

Before I had time to turn off the engine Linda was on the doorstep looking radiant in an aquamarine cashmere cardigan, a present we gave her the previous Christmas.

Linda in 2006

An aroma of freshly brewed coffee invited me into her front room and, for the first half hour, we chatted non-stop about her recent holiday to Brighton and the IT course she was determined to master to put her skills to the test on her newly acquired computer before, as she said, 'it was too late'.

'So, what's the sudden rush to find out about Blanche and Victor?' She turned to face me.

'I don't often mention my father I know, like it's a taboo subject, but I need to delve into his background. I can't sleep thinking about him.'

'Well, I'm glad you've come because I've been waiting to have a chat with you. It's been playing on my mind. I had intended to say something when I came to stay at your place back in May, but it never seemed the right moment. I know your mother never filled you in on anything. She said it was wiser in case you took sides, but I didn't agree with her. I think you should have been able to make up your own mind. Certainly, as you grew up, it seemed only right you knew all the facts.'

I felt relieved that she appeared willing to talk.

'If the truth be known, I think your father terrified your mother, afraid of what he may do if he knew she'd said something. You know what a temper he had on him. Not that she ever mentioned anything to me, but I did wonder whether he'd made her promise never to say a word to you or anyone else for that matter. That's me surmising of course, but I wouldn't be surprised.'

I couldn't wait to hurl my burning question.

'So, where *did* my parents first meet Connie? I've a vague recollection it's from way back but that's all I know.'

'Well, it's from the war days!'

'And?'

'Your parents were married … no more than a couple of years and like everybody during the war, they'd often attend the NAAFI dances in the village hall … Wolverhampton, I think it was. Navy, Army and Air Force Institute,' she rattled off, making sure I knew what the initials stood for.

'Everyone looked forward to them. Women wore their black-market nylons and with the troops they'd jitterbug the night away to Glen Miller. You could hardly see through the fog of cigarette smoke and your shoes stuck to the floor with spilled beer, but nobody cared. Now this was where they went one evening and Connie happened to be there with her boyfriend.'

'I never knew that.'

'They met up, the four of them, just as friends, but after a while, I understand Connie finished with her army chap.'

'And then what happened?' I wiped my clammy palms on my jeans.

'Well, like I said, they were friends but your father had kept in touch because in spite of your mother having to work one particular weekend – it was in the offices at the Rotherwas Munitions Factory where they filled the ammunition with explosives – he seemed to think he could take himself off to one of these dances on his own. And who do you think was there? *Connie!*' Linda thumped her clenched fist on the arm of her settee.

I stared at her over the top of my glasses.

'She was a bit of a glamour puss … high cheek bones like a model and sparkling brown eyes, because I did meet her once, I remember. I assume it was pre-arranged, the fact she was there.

But what was he playing at, because your parents were married?'

'And Mum didn't know?'

Linda shook her head. 'I think she'd have been powerless even if she had. Your father had such a confident air about him. The type who'd stand out in a crowd. The complete opposite to Blanche's delicate nature.'

'So that's where they all met?' My mouth was dry as I asked the wretched question.

'That's where they all met,' Linda repeated as she let out a sigh. I wondered what was going through her mind.

As a picture of those early days was beginning to emerge, I began to realize how little I knew and just how much I needed to know.

Linda topped up my coffee. 'Sad, when you look back.'

I shook my head in disbelief, part of me dismissive but knowing that with Linda's agile memory, everything would be accurate.

'And what about poor Mum?' I wiggled myself towards the edge of my seat as I spared a thought for this genteel lady caught up in such a hideous situation. 'What was her reaction when she found out?'

'Furious. You can imagine. I know Blanche was attractive, but I think she could see competition. What possessed the man?' Linda was in full swing. 'And it didn't stop there!'

I got up and paced around the room.

'Now, you know your father's parents had Tenby House in Hereford? The guesthouse. Well, on another of his off-duty weekends, he invited Connie to stay there. The audacity of it! Again, Blanche couldn't go because she had to work. But *she* still went. Mother and I were disgusted.'

Linda's voice became shrill as she recounted events. 'So sad for Blanche. Knowing your father, you can imagine the argument it caused. She lost pounds with all the worry and ended up going into that ghastly psychiatric place at Holm Lacy for pioneering treatment, I remember. Her nerves were in a terrible state. I mean, why would your father want to invite Connie to his parents' place. And what did they think was going on, for goodness sake?'

'So, when exactly did she arrive in Cape Town?' I felt a

pressing urge to discover more.

'That was the first thing your mother tried to establish. Seems she'd been there a couple of weeks before you got back! Your grandma wasted no time letting me know she'd arrived safely and off-loading her news. She said that although you and your mother chatted incessantly on the journey home, your father had gone quiet, no doubt wondering how best to mention you had this person staying.' Linda's voice became louder as she recounted the event. 'Apparently, all he could do was puff nervously on his cigarettes until my mother told him she'd always remembered him as talkative. That's when it all came pouring out. Poor Blanche was horrified.' Linda paused for a couple of seconds. 'And he admitted he'd already driven Connie round the peninsula to show her all the sights. Did you ever!'

Linda explained that, after my parents' arrival in Cape Town, whenever Connie's name came into conversation it always gave grounds for trouble and the stress it had caused when my mother made the uncomfortable discovery that my father had kept in touch with her. To begin with, she addressed her letters to my father's office, there was no denying that, but when the correspondence started to arrive at their home, addressed to them both, my mother began to feel less anxious. And, it seemed, Connie had referred to one day visiting them. Although uneasy about the situation, Linda said, my mother speculated whether a holiday would be the end of her communication. And as the months rolled by, things became quieter and when letters ceased arriving altogether, her vivid imagination stopped playing tricks on her.

Linda went on to tell me that with our pending trip to England, all thoughts of this person had vanished. Until the journey home, when Blanche could not believe what she was hearing. My father tried to explain that we were in England when Connie wrote to say she would be arriving and was quick to remind my mother that she had agreed she would be welcome for a holiday.

'But as Blanche pointed out, it was more Victor's idea than hers and certainly not while she was away. Couldn't the woman have waited till you were back? Ruined your homecoming, that's for sure.'

Linda talked without drawing breath. 'And your mother was always telling me theirs was the most perfect life anyone could wish for and how happy she and your father were, which I believe was true. That's why I could never understand why he was playing with fire. But Blanche was no match for him. I think he knew she wouldn't be able to stand up to him. And as for Connie … I'd have torn her hair out.' Linda's peach complexion was now deep crimson. She leaned forward to touch me on the knee, like it was an apology for my father's outrageous behaviour.

Linda remembered my mother's journey home being a nightmare. The elation she felt had evaporated, the excitement at having her own mother staying destroyed and the trust in her husband questioned. Lost for words, she pondered whether Connie's appearance on the scene, which was no doubt orchestrated by my father, had coincided with Grandma's holiday to cushion the blow.

Something else I learnt from Linda was that her mother had concerns about the family my mother was marrying into.

'Dead against it, she was.' Her ambitious standards stemmed from working in service as head housekeeper to the daughter of the Earl and Countess of Lowry Corry, Lady Blanche King King, who she named my mother after. The property, she said, was a grand affair with twelve servants. Born in the 1880s when Queen Victoria was still on the throne, my grandparents had striven hard to achieve a respectable standard of living. Alfred, my grandfather, had served his apprenticeship under a Swiss firm to become a master baker and a live-in nanny was employed to look after their three girls. During those early years, my mother and her elder sister, Freda, received a private education, my mother the more reserved, unlike her sisters, who, by Linda's own admission, were tomboys.

Linda took pride in telling me that Fanny and Alfred were well groomed; moustachioed Alfred always sported a bowler, while Fanny never ventured out without her fashionable hat, gold jewellery and gloves to accessorise her outfit.

Diane's Grandparents Fanny and Alfred, circa 1910

She said my grandfather had a placid nature and favoured a more relaxed approach to life; it was Fanny who possessed the brains, taking charge of the business accounts as Alfred showed his sympathetic side all too often, always willing to wipe the slate when customers owed money on the bread round. That's when Fanny would point out to him in her efficient manner that to make ends meet there was no way he could run a business like that.

Theirs was a loving and cheerful home, one where everyone towed the line and as they gathered round the meal table at the end of the day, Alfred would recount tales of his deliveries with his horse and trap while Fanny entertained them on her mandolin.

As they were growing up, what the girls loved most was the exhilaration of their uncle Charlie driving them through the streets of Hereford in his open topped motorcar. Well educated, Fanny's brother had landed an excellent job at the local Council Offices and back in those days was one of the few proud owners of a car. Put to the test, she couldn't recall the make except that it had big shiny headlamps on either side, although she remembered that with his love of adventure they would often lose their way down leafy narrow lanes and once out in the open country-side he would put his foot down, press the horn and tell them to hold on to their bonnets and when anything resembled a hill, they would have to get out and walk.

From left Blanche, Freda and Linda (seated), Christmas 1928

When it was the turn for Fanny's children to marry, she was determined that they should stand by the standards she and Alfred had striven to achieve. She considered my father to be from 'the wrong side of the street'. The eldest of three children, he lived with his brother, Billy, and sister, Nancy, at Tenby House in King Street, Hereford, the former residence of the priest from the local Catholic Church, where his parents, Annie, and William ran a guesthouse. William was a painter and decorator and Annie a cook, but it was her 'slovenly' appearance that Fanny disliked. However, the main reason for her disapproval was their differ-ence in faith; with my father's family Roman Catholic and Fanny's Church of England she was convinced it would lead to problems.

Victor and Blanche with his parents, Annie and William, and sister Nancy, 1942

I felt relieved to have my aunt on my side; her astonishing candour surprised me as though she wanted me to know every detail. It seemed absurd to be having this discussion with her but think she could sense my frustration and my eagerness to piece events together from decades ago. Not only had I squeezed her dry for answers to my quick-fire questioning, but I now felt I had a clearer understanding of those early years. It was hard to believe that the person I was talking about was my father: I wanted every-thing to be rosy and innocent.

I downed the rest of my coffee as I contemplated the reality. 'I never thought I'd be having this chat with you,' Linda admit-ted. She flopped back against her cream cushions and appeared thankful we were able to have such a frank conversation.

I hoped my talk with her was the start of wanting to offload my inner secret.

As Linda darted from pillar to post about those early war days, she warned me that her generation were getting a bit thin on the ground. 'So, if you think of anything else to ask, you'd better fire away while you can!'

I looked at my watch. We had talked non-stop for the best part of the morning. 'Don't leave it too late getting back,' she said. So, after a quick lunch I bid her farewell but as I reversed out of her drive she rushed into the garden and waved both arms for me to stop. 'I'll rack my brains and see what else I can come up with,' she shouted.

I made sure I was out of sight before stopping the car to mop my stinging eyes.

My brain pounded for the duration of my journey home. I told myself not to be ridiculous but with so much on my mind I knew that if I wasn't to disclose my findings to Chris, I would have to pretend my visit to Cheltenham had been just like any other.

I felt relieved to be back in my own home but the minute I opened the front door the phone was ringing. It was normal for me to call Linda to say I was home safely, but she was ringing me.

'I wasn't sure you'd be back, but I couldn't wait to speak. The second you left I shot upstairs and found a bundle of Blanche's letters tucked in an old briefcase at the back of my wardrobe. Ones she'd sent from South Africa. Not all of them, of course, but I have a wad of them. I knew they were somewhere but didn't dare say anything while you were here, in case I couldn't put my hand on them. I must have had them half a century. It's so long ago I'm wondering why I've saved some and not others. Before I send them to you, I'm going to sit down with a cuppa and have a read.'

Linda appeared thrilled with her find. 'And I've been thinking. You know Connie's friend Freda had a daughter, Judy. Well, have you thought about talking to her? See if she can offer you any insight into her background.'

Freda and Connie had been lifelong friends, so Judy would have known her since she was a little girl. It had never occurred to me, but now Linda had mentioned it, it seemed a sensible idea. I would make contact and see whether she knew of any skeletons in the cupboard, but that would have to wait. I had heard enough for one day.

My mind spun with these new revelations.

And letters! Their existence had never crossed my mind.

The meeting with Linda had given me an emotional battering I had not bargained for.

I lay in bed that night mulling over the events. I imagined I knew everything about my parents' background, but I had been wrong. My heart pounded as I thought about my remarkable mother and my controlling father. I knew now what a pivotal role he had played in the lives of both my mother and Connie.

As dawn broke, I swung my legs out of bed and took myself downstairs to tackle the long overdue hoovering, slamming my Dyson into the skirting boards. I was still as wild as I had been the day before.

'Why all the noise?' Chris bellowed from upstairs.

'Nothing!' I wiped the beads of perspiration from my top lip with the back of my hand. Still in my pyjamas, I was on a mission. I needed to unearth photographs that had not seen daylight since God knows when. Clutching a mug of strong black coffee, I plonked myself down in the conservatory with an armful of albums in the hope they would shed further light on those early years.

My stomach flipped, knowing I was about to clap eyes on my father after all this time. I opened the book and there he was, his strong features clean shaven and youthful. With his semi-serious expression, he stood proud in army uniform, his feet astride, military hat clutched in his left hand, his dark chocolate hair cut Army short. The date underneath was 1940. I had seen this photograph countless times before but, after my conversation with Linda, I was studying him in a different light. I needed to establish what made this man tick and to understand what possessed him to behave the way he did.

As I scoured the photographs for clues, I came across six small snapshots of Connie in different poses grouped together on a page of their own and another of her in a hammock looking playful with her leg in the air. I sat there mystified. I had come across these before, although at the time it never occurred to me to wonder why they were in our family album.

Flicking through, I found a fine assortment of faded sepia pictures dating back decades; some my father had clustered together from 1936 when he and my mother were on holiday in Weymouth in their first flush of romance. He's striding upright along the seafront with my mother a pace behind, looking relaxed and smiling. He had even written witty comments under each one in his copperplate hand. I wished the photographs could speak so I could hear what he had to say, whether his life was happy or sad, awkward or difficult and, if he could live it over again, whether he might conduct it in a different way.

Hundreds of Kodak glossy prints and transparencies littered the floor. Sifting through, I discovered another black and white picture, now jagged at the edges with age. It was a graphic image of my parents. Taken before I was born, their faces were as I remembered. They were standing together on the sloping banks of the picturesque River Wye, holding hands as they gazed tenderly into one another's eyes. My mother's hour-glass figure and my father's young innocent looks tugged at my heart. It transported me back to my mother's tales of their happy teenage days, a blissful image I wanted to cherish and hold on to.

I found it strange when we had our little chats how it was always my mother and never my father who talked about the good old days. Her blue eyes glistened as she recounted what a smasher he was, and I remember her words – 'a real catch' – because I visualised her plucking him from the sea. With a sadness in her voice, she explained about their frugal wedding with no bridesmaids and only a handful of family as others were away on active service and with rationing how she'd saved her clothing coupons to purchase a deep turquoise suit off-set with chocolate brown hat and shoes.

'But I felt exhilarated, knowing Victor was all mine. Looked like a film star, he did'.

Studying the photographs, I had become fixated with my super daddy. It brought a lump to my throat as I reflected on those early years, when the two of us wallowed in precious times together, his blue-eyed, blond-haired little girl snuggled on his lap on our sun-bleached veranda in Claremont. I revelled in his attention with repeated requests to read the story of Orlando, a marmalade cat who got up to all kinds of tricks, with the added attraction that Blanche was the name of one of her kittens. With his limitless patience he did his best to put into simple words how the earth rotated on legs, like a ballet dancer pirouetting through light and dark once every twenty four hours, his tongue in his cheek with concentration as he sketched his explanation on the cover of an old flimsy blue atlas.

I adored being in his company and when he returned home at the end of the day he'd scoop me into his muscular arms, his harsh toughened skin coarse against mine as he carried me around the estate – he referred to our garden as his estate – with both of us eager to catch a glimpse of Flash, our quick as lightening scaly lizard whose home was amongst the spiky cacti in our rockery.

Looking at the pictures all these years later left me with complicated feelings, knowing how my father had behaved towards my mother. Those early fun days we spent together in the golden sunshine were endless but underneath the surface his 'super daddy' image had vanished.

Diane Harding

CHAPTER 6
A ROLLER COASTER
EXISTENCE

Connie's initial weeks of planned holiday had turned into months. Our unexpected visitor had become well ensconced and with an established routine taking shape, I revelled in her company. She was someone I had fun with and involved in my open-all-hours sweet shop. My library was another regular event with the tickets I had made for my books stamped when taken out and slotted back into the system when returned.

Connie slept in the guest bedroom. Painted a soothing shade of eau de nil, in one corner was a glass topped kidney-shaped dressing table with a chintz frill, in the other a cream wicker chair and in the middle of the parquet floor a brightly coloured rug that my father had haggled over with an Indian trader soon after arriving in the country.

For me, a highlight was to perch on her much-travelled brown trunk to observe her applying her makeup. With a hand mirror angled to the light, the first performance was to ease saucer-shaped glass contact lenses into each eye. Eyebrows came next, followed by mascara which she applied with a brush and a block of black paste that she would spit on to soften after which she painted her lips with a glossy red lipstick taken from a crocodile skin makeup bag. Always in that order, the scent sprayed behind each ear from a pink glass atomiser that sat on her dressing table the final ritual. Her jolly voice and a smile that stretched from ear to ear invited me into her world and on pocket money day, she would happily drop pennies into my black and gold piggy bank.

My mother and Connie were two opposites; my mother with her jet-black hair swept back in a bun had a natural beauty, unlike Connie, where appearances were everything. My mother was sensitive to others, quiet and content, whereas Connie was flamboyant with a vast collection of earrings that always held my attention and when she wore high heels, she towered over my diminutive mother.

If we were not venturing on a family outing together, Auntie Connie would suggest we go it alone. She never referred to me as Diane but would grab my hand and say, 'Come on Di Di.' With her enormous white rimmed sunglasses, she would escort me to my favourite sweet shop, always stopping at the end of our road to admire an elderly gentleman's garden with a display of trees he'd snipped into exotic bird shapes. Running on ahead, I'd stand outside that archaic shop and wait for Connie to catch me up. As we entered, an old-fashioned doorbell jangled and through a curtain at the rear would emerge an old lady, bent double and dumpy. Jars of sweets of all colours lined the shelves and the magical smell of candy and treacle in that little shop made my taste buds tingle. Connie allowed me to choose whatever I liked, with everything weighed and shaken into paper bags just like my toy shop back home. It was also normal for her to pop a tube of Spangles in her handbag for later and she always bought long strips of liquorice as a surprise for my father as these were his favourite, but I never recall a treat for my mother.

With highlights in her hair and a personality that fizzed like lemonade, at the age of thirty-one she seemed to fit surprisingly well into our daily routine and cosy family life. I adored my new playmate although, from what I observed, my mother did not appear too pleased; there was always laugher between my father and Connie, but I heard little from my mother. Perhaps she resented the amount of time I spent in her company.

For all the occasions we had together, few memories of being alone with my father spring to mind but the rare times we shared were irreplaceable, especially when I accompanied him on his routine visits to customers. Once home, he allowed me to stand on an old wooden box alongside him at his garage workbench to help sort through the grub infested and heat damaged chocolate collected on his rounds. As fast as I removed the wrappers, he packaged into bundles anything in edible condition to dole out to the deprived children in their shanty towns. He said the delight on their faces was a joy; like squirrels with nuts, they scurried off squealing. The intense smell of chocolate lingered for days after those sessions and even now spirals me back to those unforgettable times. I was never happier than when I was in his company; during those early years of growing up this is how I knew and loved him.

As time went by, Connie had fallen in love with the area and with full time employment took advantage of my father's daily chauffeuring to and from the Old Mutual building in Cape Town down by the state-of-the-art foreshore. Working gave her an independent lifestyle, leaving my mother to do what she did best; to care for me, cook and run the home with the help of our servant.

To enquire who our guest was and why she was living with us never occurred to me. I accepted her continued presence. To me, she was my auntie Connie and what she lacked in her own family she made up for with mine. To outsiders, my mother and Connie appeared to get on well with one another, although, looking back, my mother must have despaired, knowing she showed no sign of leaving. Powerless to change the regime and too frightened to express her bitterness, it must have been a case of putting her wrath to one side whilst trying to make light of an intolerable situation.

For me, Saturdays were extra special. With me wedged between the pair of them, we'd wait at the local station to catch the electric cabled train into Cape Town for elevenses either at the Waldorf, where glowing table lamps gave a cosy feel to the restaurant, or Stuttafords departmental store; when hot air gushed out from the pavement gratings onto my legs, I knew we'd arrived. Pushing through the heavy double doors, past perfumes where Connie always presented her wrist for a tester, and up the escalator to the top floor, we queued to be seated; for the ladies, it was coffee and buttered tea cakes, for me it was an ice cream soda served in a tall glass with a long-handled spoon.

It was during one of these visits that I succeeded in shutting down the entire escalator system. I had trailed my hand along the shiny rail until it disappeared into the black brushes at the base, but I'd followed it too far and it became trapped amongst the machinery.

'Stop the escalator!' my mother yelled. 'Her hand. She's going to lose it.'

The shop was in chaos with Chinese whispers ricocheting through menswear. A sea of faces gathered round. There was noisy chatter. A kaleidoscope of colours flashed before my eyes. I came around in my mother's arms to find the medical staff checking to make sure I could return home.

On another of these visits, it was my turn to come to Connie's rescue when she mislaid one of her contact lenses. It happened on the pavement outside the store. Teaming with passers by the ladies cordoned off the area where hawk eye, a nickname she had given me because she said I never missed a thing, scrabbled on all fours and managed to find it.

By the time I turned five, nothing had changed. Auntie Connie had made our home her home. It was never enough for my father to invite her to join us for the occasional trip to the beach or cinema. She accompanied us on every outing. I could never understand why and because she had been living with us for two years, I sensed my mother was livid that she had still not packed her bags and returned to England. Tutting was her most effective weapon but a trait that infuriated my father. Whenever heated discussions occurred between my parents, the misery in my mother's eyes made my heart melt but wrapping her arms around me like a protective cloak for my sake she would keep home life on as even a keel as possible. Even now, I can smell the intensity of her Yardley's Lily of the Valley talc.

It wasn't long after my fifth birthday that my mother explained that I would be starting something called kindergarten. Held in St. Stephen's Church Hall, it was a short walk from home. I jumped for joy at the prospect of making new friends but my first morning was a frightening experience. Because it was a place I knew nothing about, I tugged at my mother's skirt and begged her not to leave. I remember a dozen or so children sitting round the perimeter of a claustrophobic room with white-haired

Miss Pratt perched on a high stool, her enormous feet dangling from long skinny legs. Discipline was important and we sat in silence, unless required to chant the alphabet or numbers by rote. My knees knocked when it was my turn to read from the Janet and John book. Unable to make out one of the words I incurred her wrath. Hot tears filled my eyes and I hated everything about the place. Horrible boys added to my inferiority when one playtime they dragged me indoors laughing after I had snagged my nose on a rusty barbed wire fence. The ancient Miss Beck, whose role it was to bash away at the ivories during our singing lessons and who had a strange leg that made a clonking sound as she walked, patched me up.

It was here I spent the precursor days to my big school.

With my father in charge of the Cadbury depot in Cape Town, it always fell upon my parents to entertain overseas guests or visiting company directors. And, whether for business or pleasure, my father's coastline tours to soak up the rugged peaks of Table Mountain and the perilous cliffs that plunged into the ocean took priority, including Lions Head and Signal Hill where at night the city lights twinkled below like jewels.

Whenever Mr Cadbury visited, this was the routine, followed by a luncheon at home. Looking back, knowing Connie would be at work, I wonder if it was a midday invitation to spare my father the embarrassment of having to explain her presence. For days before these anticipated arrivals, there would be a frantic kerfuffle in the kitchen; with silverware polished and our special dinner service brought out from the top cupboard. Strict instructions followed. 'Whatever you do,' my mother would say, 'don't mention you've not seen the china before. Won't look good. Besides, Mr Cadbury might think it only sees daylight on special occasions,' which, of course, I knew to be true.

At the time of one of these visits, we had a dog called Rex, a cross between a Rhodesian Ridgeback and Great Dane. He was like a docile donkey and adorable. But this day, his placid temperament turned into mischievousness. He had taken a liking to Mr Cadbury's grey trilby; bolting off with it into the back garden; with his playful tooth marks, he punctured the fabric and reduced his hat to a sieve. I remember my mother panicking, my father looking worried and me fleeing out of sight.

I was not a spoilt child; what I wanted and what I got were different things, but two longings spring to mind. The first wish was a Wendy house where I could open the front door, draw back red check curtains, and entertain people with drinks from my china tea service. Knowing my father could construct it with his woodwork talents, I fantasised over this more than anything, but it never materialised. However, my second yearning did come true: hula hoops were all the craze and borrowing my friend Shirley's from next door, I found I'd mastered the art of swinging it around my waist hundreds of times without stopping. I begged for one and the evening my father returned from work carrying a pale pink hoop I thought I was the luckiest girl in the world.

I also remember trying to emulate Connie's stiff petticoats. The height of fashion in the Fifties, I paraded like a grown-up with scrunched-up newspaper under my gathered skirt to give the desired effect of layers of stiff netting. I felt a million dollars with my antics, which became a source of amusement to everyone.

Despite my mother not working, she was smart and fashionable. She and Connie devoted hours to dressmaking and with my mother's Singer machine working overtime it was nothing unusual to see our lounge carpet strewn with pattern pieces, tailor's chalk, measuring tape and yards of pretty fabric. The pair of them also attached huge importance to the sending and receiving of letters and with our oak bureau stocked full of flimsy blue airmails, the writing ritual usually took place at weekends.

For my mother to confide in Linda had become a lifeline. And it was in one of these letters she informed her:

> 'Vic and I went to a party on Thursday and I wore the black bra you sent me for the first time. Good fit. Connie wasn't invited. Thoroughly enjoyed myself!'

Blanche and Victor, 1954

In another letter dated October 1954 she wrote:

'I save all I can, but you know it adds up slowly.'

And then:

'I feel laden with grief and unbearable thoughts. It's all too much for me at times.'

Galloping towards my sixth birthday it was time for me to leave kindergarten for the real thing. I would be attending Springfield Convent for day girls; the Catholic education my mother had vowed she would abide by.

Springfield Convent

Dress rehearsals in my new navy tunic and blue striped tie became the norm and with a special bus to deliver us to and from school every day, my heart pounded at the thought of the looming adventure.

As I waited at the bus stop on that first morning, I gripped my mother's arm as apprehension mixed with high spirits. Secure in the knowledge she would be there to meet me on my return, I hugged her goodbye. With his flat black cap and a jovial smile, the driver welcomed his exuberant children on board. The bus was a bone shaker and during the short journey that seemed to take forever, he crunched through the gears at regular intervals until he swung his hoard of chattering children into the winding school drive. In the distance, I spied an impressive, white-washed building with a wrought-iron veranda. While the theatrical arm-waving Mother Superior scurried to greet her new fledglings, other nuns glided towards us, their black habits swishing, and all trace of hair hidden by face hugging wimples.

The new recruits had lessons in a block of classrooms away from the main campus, where bright sunlight shafted through high sash windows. The playground was a concrete yard with outside toilets, often blocked and reeking, so to make it home without needing a pee was always a bonus.

My first classroom was enormous. Our wooden desks had lift-up lids with ink wells in the top right corner and arranged in tiered rows, it allowed the teacher at the front to keep a vigilant eye. I will never forget Sister Francis, my first teacher, whose saintly exterior was a decoy for her authoritarian approach. We adhered to a strict regime, something I learnt the hard way when I disobeyed the no talking rule. In a flash, I was in front of the class, hauled over her knee and reprimanded with a firm hand on my derriere.

Worshipping in church was a regular event. We snaked our way through the school grounds in crocodile fashion and chanted Hail Marys before reverently dipping our fingers in the holy water to mark the sign of the cross on our foreheads upon entering. My time there taught me obedience and good manners but also to fear hellfire and damnation. I enrolled in ballet and tennis lessons played with short-handled racquets and to prevent the loss of mine my father commissioned the Cadbury's window-dresser to engrave my name in red and gold on the rim. I was in my element with these activities, but my biggest dread was the swimming lessons. Lined up, the teacher coaxed us girls into the pool and with a rope around our waists towed us through uninviting olive-green water. But the lunchtime tuck shops more than compensated, something not regarded as healthy today. With twelve old pennies to a shilling back then, two pence of my pocket money bought a bag of gob stoppers and liquorice pipes.

It wasn't long after I'd started at the Convent that I discovered my father was planning a trip to England.

My mother wrote to Linda in October 1955 to give her the news:

'V is saving up this year's holiday for he hopes to visit his people next January. C isn't due for any because of her last trip. She had planned to go home again about February because her mother was so much worse, but she had a telegram last week to say her mother has passed away with a cancer of the bowel. Now she will have no incentive to go to England at all. It was rather sudden I believe.

Unfortunately, my maid left in November. I thought I might manage without one until after V gets back, for I shall have less to do, with no awful shirts to wash and iron and he is so fussy about meals. He sails on 6th January and due here 1st March. At the moment I feel in need of a holiday, for apart from having far more to do the weather is much hotter. Diane brought home some very good test papers from school and also her best report of the year. What a pity V is visiting England in winter – as you can imagine he is sure not to get a good impression, especially in Hereford. Cheerio dear, much love B xx'

Next was her news in February 1956:

'We had a quiet Xmas with a lovely turkey, pudding etc. We had John to dinner, so it helped to even things up. He is from Wales but out here on business, lives in digs in our road and V met him at a meeting one night so he is a frequent visitor. He is about 33 and quite a nice fellow but, unfortunately, C is not a bit interested. V gave me a beautiful hand carved Stinkwood jewel box and some brilliant earrings. Diane gave me a bulldog charm for my bracelet. Diane and I are here on holiday, just for a week. It's a guest farm – 300 acres – about 50 miles from Cape Town at a place called Franschhoek. I have a new maid who can't cook, so don't know how they will fare back at home, but I'm not worried. It's a lovely place here, very quiet and I felt I could do with a little relaxation. I do wish you were here for like you I get very lonely and know no-one…. You must excuse handwriting but I'm doing this in the beautiful gardens and can hear various conversations all round. Lovely swimming pool here. Much love Blanche and Diane xxxxxx'

From the gist of these informative letters, it appeared that my mother's visits to the tranquillity of Excelsior Farm at Franschhoek held the short-term solution to her recovery.

Whenever I heard mention of the farm, my excitement spiralled. In the eyes of a young child it was paradise, a secret place where we enjoyed time together. Surrounded by stillness the weather was always sunny. Apart from the inviting blue waters of the swimming pool, there were new grounds to explore and if it was milking time, I'd follow the shady path down to the weather-beaten parlour to watch the cows being milked by hand, a place I could smell before I arrived. And my mother would do what she had come for; forget about home, calm her warring nerves, and enjoy a gripping novel whilst relaxing in the shade of the sweet-smelling pines. I adored these holidays. It was a time for unfettered fun and when one holiday ended, I longed for the next to begin.

Later that year my mother reported to Linda:

> 'I wish we could come back to England for it would make things much easier for me.'

My father had a wicked sense of humour and was a master at spinning yarns. The life and soul of any gathering, he would have us in fits with his ridiculous tales and as the evening grew older, so the bursts of laughter grew louder. An avid reader, he was familiar with anything and everything there was to know about the Great War and always keen to reminisce about his own experiences including the one about him on a route march during his time as sergeant in the Second World War when he'd stopped to buy cigarettes and left the squad to march on ahead and then had to hop on a bus to catch up with them. I concluded he must have been daring back then.

In another letter my mother explained:

> 'There have been six cases of smallpox in Cape Town, so the public have been advised to be vaccinated and centres have been organised. It's not compulsory but we went last Monday to our own Doctor.'

I will never forget that unpleasant experience. A long queue of anxious patients snaked their way up a flight of stone stairs to the doctor's surgery on the first floor. As we waited for the door to open to admit the next patient, my uncontrollable sobs outraged my father to such an extent that he snatched a handful of my hair and dragged me up the stairs screaming, while my mother pleaded with him not to be so cruel.

She wrote again in February 1956:

> 'It does seem a pity that Vic had to come over during the

winter. I'm afraid what ideas he might have had re a transfer will be dashed after the Arctic conditions prevailing in England at present. Evidently, it's been the worst winter for fifty years I've read. It's very upsetting really, when you think Vic hasn't seen any of my relations. I just don't understand him, or why he is so peculiar. However, I will see what he has to say on his return – he sails this Thursday. It's been quite peaceful without him and of course much less work and some food I like for a change.

I expect Mother has told you I now have a Hoover vacuum cleaner.

Much love, Blanche xxxx'

Life was like a rollercoaster and for all the downs we enjoyed light-hearted moments when everyone wore a smile and laughter filled the air. One of these occasions was at Connie's expense when she and my parents had been talking to our policeman neighbour, Peter Dodd, by the overhanging granadilla vines (passion fruits) that trailed along a sturdy wooden trellis at the far end of the garden. Eager for a better view she hauled herself onto the slatted wooden lid covering my father's special liquid manure housed in an elongated metal drum. But there was a deafening crack when the cover gave way plunging her neck deep into the slimy substance containing the secret ingredient my father swore by. With the aid of a ladder she emerged coated in a mahogany slurry and as my father hosed her down, I doubted anyone could laugh so much. My mother said it was the best entertainment she'd had in a long time.

Another occasion was when my mother and Connie had taken to their beds with a virus and my father thought he would try his hand in the kitchen. He knew how to boil a kettle but that was all, so when he announced that Welsh rarebit would do the trick for the two ladies everyone expressed surprise.

'How d'you make this stuff?' he asked Bertha, our new maid, who, at sixteen, was bashful and clueless about culinary matters.

Diane with Bertha in the back garden, 1956

'Not sure Master. Madam usually does it.' My mother shouted instructions from the bedroom, staggered to think he had contemplated the task. With his chest puffed out and a fine balancing act he paraded his offering down the hallway; but lively Rex, our horse-like great Dane, bounded up behind him causing the Welsh rarebit to take to the air like flying saucers. Determined not to waste his efforts he peeled the adhered mass off the hall runner with Bertha and I clutching our sides as we witnessed the performance.

From time to time, when my father got cross and arguments flared, my mother would say she felt 'peculiar'. It was her favourite word. I had no idea why this should be or what was wrong with her and, from what I observed, I don't think Connie noticed anything either. I never heard her enquire how she was feeling, nor, for that matter, did my father and when my mother's nerves got the better of her, she would escape to her bedroom and lie down.

One of these instances occurred when my parents had received an invitation to a black-tie ball. It was at the prestigious Mount Nelson hotel in Cape Town. I wanted to know what they would do with the ball and my mother chuckled. She said it was a charity event and that she would be wearing her long gown with dancing after dinner. It was nothing unusual to see her slinky figure looking glamorous in her strapless attire of deep fuchsia taffeta overlaid with delicate black lace that rustled as she twirled. With a twinkling diamante necklace and matching dangling earrings and black satin platform shoes unearthed from a box kept in the bottom of her wardrobe, it was as though she had walked off a film set. 'Yippee,' I'd shout; whenever they saw daylight that meant I could teeter round in them the following day.

But uneasiness had been simmering, with Connie the culprit.

I remember the date. It was the sixth of March. It was my mother's thirty-eighth birthday. And she had requested to accompany my father alone.

'Vic, please. Just for once.' I recall the words clearly.

'Connie's coming!' he told her. It was the first time I had seen tears of disappointment in my mother's eyes.

Broad-shouldered and upright, my father entered the lounge in his black dinner jacket, a cream cummerbund hugging his waist and matching silk scarf with delicate tassels slung round his neck. When Connie emerged in a flowing scarlet gown and glittering earrings that framed her high cheek bones, my mother let out a wail.

Connie in her finery

She had made no attempt to prepare herself; instead, we remained huddled together in the rattan armchair with me clutching my rag doll for comfort. The disagreement continued as she begged my father not to behave like a lunatic. Her body trembled against mine as she tried to persuade him. It was a rare display.

'Come on,' said my father, as he adjusted his bow tie in the mirror. He ushered Connie towards the door but not before his parting shot. 'Have this!' he bellowed, as my mother's birthday present hurtled towards her like a fast cricket ball towards a wicket. And with his deliverance, the door slammed, and my father did not even kiss me goodbye.

'Take no notice darling. Daddy's in a bad mood.'

My father's fearsome ways that evening made an enormous

impression on me. Over the years I have tried to erase the terrifying ordeal from my mind, but the occasion and harsh words have
made the scene impossible to forget. It was outrageous to think
that Connie should take the place of my mother and obvious that
both she and my father had little regard for the hurt they were
inflicting. When I think back, it's impossible to imagine the jealousy my mother must have felt.

Apart from these outbursts triggering my mother's unhappiness, it also prompted my urge to leave home. Rushing to my
bedroom, I would empty the books from a small brown suitcase
with worn leather protectors and cram in the dolls that I hoped
would keep me company. Hauling my load through the kitchen,
I'd perch on the back-veranda step and announce in a loud voice
that I was off, although where, I had no idea.

'I don't think it's a sensible idea,' my mother would say to
me with that warm tender smile of hers. 'And besides, darling, I'll
miss you.' I spent a great deal of time on that doorstep, miserable
and confused. I often wonder whether it was a cry for help or
whether I was trying to make my father take notice that, if he
didn't behave, I'd be gone but the effect his moods were having
on me was obvious.

In May 1957, my mother sounded dejected and in one of her
letters to Linda was pleading for advice:

> 'It's all such a problem and I've thought and thought until
> ideas have chased round and round in my head and I don't
> quite know what to do for the best. Even if I can't bring
> Diane, I do think I should come home this year. I can't
> quite understand why Vic is so against it, but I really think
> he is worried in case I decide to stay. I don't really think he
> knows what he wants, for he feels very unsettled over here
> at times and talks of asking Cadbury's for a transfer and
> then he thinks he is better off in South Africa. If I decide to
> come this year, it doesn't leave much time to do part time
> work before I come but I have offered to work in England
> for my return fare.'

She then went on to talk about getting legal aid or a court order, I
assume with the idea of leaving my father, which indicated that

the situation at home was dire:

> 'I can't think why it should be so complicated for me, but I would love to see you to talk things over and as you suggest, perhaps we could work things out. There is a boat coming from Australia to England belonging to the Shaw Saville line on her last voyage before she is broken up. I wondered whether I might get a berth on that when she sails in early June. I should hate to leave Diane. My love to you Linda and Mother if she is with you and do give me any advice or suggestions if you can.
> Much love Blanche xx'

Although my mother's longed-for trip to England in 1957 did not materialise, that same year I transferred into my next class, unaware how soon my time at the Convent would end.

My Sunday School had presented me with a book for regular attendance. I was fiercely proud of it and packed it in my little leather satchel to show my teacher. But it came under heavy scrutiny when the Mother Superior discovered I was attending a Church of England Sunday School. Communication between the Convent and my livid father began in earnest; if anyone annoyed him, he made it known. As we lined up for morning prayers, I flapped a letter he had written in front of the Nun's face. I battled to make my voice heard as I tried to explain 'Sister, this is about me being non-Catholic'. Those were my exact words and soon the wheels for my next school were set in motion.

After the long summer holidays, it was new uniform again. It was a different shade of blue and this time I liked it even more.

Diane's first day at Herschel School

Herschel School, founded by William Herschel the astronomer, is still an independent girls' school. Although I was a day pupil, it was also 'home' to boarders who came from wealthy farm owners up country and where members of staff, regardless of their marital status, were addressed as 'Miss'.

My first headmistress was Miss McLean. With cropped silver hair, she sported shapeless tweed suits and brown brogues whereas Miss Kittow, her replacement, was a younger and more flamboyant character; in a flowing black gown and mortar board she'd flounce onto the stage, place her hymn book and notices on the rostrum in front of her and stand in silence as she peered down on us girls with a beady eye. And whenever she entered the classroom, we leapt to our feet to give the customary curtsey. In my class of seventeen, there was me, Diane, a Dinah and a Diana and our often-mistaken identities proved a source of amusement. To us girls, Miss Kittow became known as Kitty, although only in soft whispers.

The imposing white-washed Cape Dutch building stood in sizeable grounds with endless corridors, a grand extensive library, and adjoining chapel. We wore tackies (plimsolls) for sport, played hockey and tennis on gravel courts and the swimming pool with its three diving boards and glinting aquamarine water was a re-freshing contrast from the misery I'd experienced at the Convent.

Herschel School

Trying to please my father with my school achievements was a challenge; the fact he had achieved so much from humble be-ginnings made it more important for me to succeed. I tried to give of my best in whatever I did but best was never good enough alt-hough, to his delight, the one subject I excelled in was languages; Latin, French and Afrikaans. He said to speak a foreign language would be beneficial, career wise. And the elocution lessons he put me through so as not to inherit the South African accent stood me in good stead. As a shy child, I blossomed, acting, and learning poems from the Christopher Robin book which I still have in my possession and treasure. I was also successful in landing the part of Cinderella in the production at prep school. Performed in the middle of the hall, which was the latest innovation for its time, my parents and Connie positioned themselves in the front row of the stage. Hoping I would make my father proud with my solo songs, my adrenalin on that first evening performance was hard to contain. The next day, my friends quizzed me about Connie but to avoid an explanation I ran off; I tried to keep her presence and the difficulties in my parents' marriage a secret from the world.

A highlight every year was the school's annual fete. Held in the grounds with a brass band to entertain the crowds it was a much-anticipated event. With the usual promise from Connie that she would like to attend, the previous evening she had eaten crab with disastrous consequences. Although she had no sleep that night and looked ashen, a disagreement with a crustacean was not going to deter her from putting on her heels so she could listen to the 'dishy men' playing their trombones; their white uniforms appeared to be the attraction.

My father was a supportive parent. Although he showed his initial displeasure, he made a financial contribution when Herschel needed a practice wall for tennis and volunteered his services to make props for the various concerts. He was generous with his flowers too. Whatever the occasion, he sent me to school laden with his prize dahlias, cut fresh that morning.

I was now eight, my mother thirty-nine and Auntie Connie was still with us. We had just celebrated Christmas Day. Everything was perfect. Santa had visited and left a metal clockwork squirrel in my stocking. Coloured paper chains hung from the lounge ceiling and an assortment of bright balloons swayed from the chandelier in a soft summer breeze. A giant Christmas tree stood in the corner of the room with a comforting aroma of fresh pine resin permeating the air. Holders with spiral wax candles were clamped to the long branches, while delicate glass baubles and strands of silver tinsel glinted in the sun's rays. On our oak sideboard, the illuminated musical church given to me by one of my father's business associates, Abe Kaye, had made its annual appearance and I wound it up every now and then for a rendition of *Silent Night*.

While the turkey turned golden in the oven, I sang along to jolly carols playing on the gramophone as the anticipation escalated at the thought of finding a silver charm in the plum pudding my mother had prepared months earlier.

But the following day, my festive fun ended without warning. Combing my hair early that morning, my mother sat me on her lap and told me she needed to go away.

Diane Harding

CHAPTER 7
MENTAL BREAKDOWN

'I've not been feeling well,' my mother explained as she sat me on her lap and held me in a tight embrace. I didn't like what I was hearing.

'I hoped it wouldn't have to come to this, but I need a break. It's my nerves. They're bad.' But that meant little to an eight-year-old. I had heard of being nervous, but 'bad' nerves; what were they? Although I had seen my mother resting in bed for weeks prior to Christmas, I had no idea why. Tears trickled as the implication began to sink in.

'Away to a hospital to make her better,' my father told me over breakfast. The suddenness of her news caused me confusion and the thought she was ill enough to go away frightened me. Alarming thoughts filled my head, knowing I would have to cope without her. Would she come back? What if something happened to her or, worse still, what if she died?

'What's wrong with her?' I asked but little explanation came my way. I thought it strange, but it never occurred to me to question why she should be feeling this way. And then I overheard something about electric shock treatment. From what I gathered it sounded terrifying.

'It'll help her forget her past,' my father said, but I could not understand why anyone would want to forget about their past.

And there was also something about agoraphobia. I had never come across that word before, but my mother said she was suffering from it.

It began to make sense. She dreaded the ten-minute stroll to our local shopping precinct; the four walls of our home had become her boundary but with my gentle persuasion and our arms linked together she'd relent although only if we made a beeline for the ladies' powder room in the departmental store the minute we arrived. Once I had settled her into the comfy armchair, I'd scurry about on my errands, queuing at Braham's the butchers for the weekend meat and at the deli opposite for gorgonzola and sweet milk cheese. Woolworths, the equivalent of Marks and Spencer, was another stop to purchase her favourite savoury crackers imported from England.

Sometimes, she would tell me her nerves were as tight as a wound-up spring, but she never elaborated. That was when I'd scoop up the bunch of dried grasses from the cream porcelain pot on her bedroom windowsill and stroke them up and down her bare arms as she tried to unwind. She would tell me that she found our little sessions therapeutic and how calm she felt afterwards but was always cautious never to mention it within earshot of my father, who thought the whole idea poppycock.

As a young child, I found the reasoning behind her abnormal bouts impossible to understand. After I had gone to bed, every so often there would be heated discussions between my parents loud enough for me to hear. And, sometimes, I would hear Connie's name mentioned, how my mother was unhappy that she was still living with us and how she had become 'rooted to our family'.

One mealtime I remember asking her, 'Haven't you got a home to go to?'

'That's not what we ask people,' my father warned with raised eyebrows. 'Now get on with your meal.' That was the last time I mentioned it.

Too private to own up to her distress and never giving away the reason for her warring nerves, my mother and I stuck together; I became sensitive to her needs and found myself doing increasingly more for her, but sadly it seemed her health had spiralled out of control with her admitted into a ghastly psychiatric hospital on that Boxing Day. Visiting my mother in the evening was a magical time and one I looked forward to. Sat alongside my father on the shiny leather bench seat of his Dodge it was just the two of us. As we neared our destination, we drove along an avenue lined with a canopy of dense mysterious fir trees where my father convinced me hundreds of fairies lived in the treetops.

I knew we had arrived when a meandering drive flanked by deep sapphire hydrangeas beckoned us. It was the one bright thing about the place. In the distance, a square grey building loomed; its very purpose made me shudder. As I counted my way up the four shallow concrete steps to a studded wooden entrance door, it was here, I glimpsed another world. The baronial hall had a cold clinical feel and smelt of disinfectant; nurses darted about in white uniforms with white caps perched upright on their heads and sometimes I'd see a doctor's white coat flapping as he scurried down a long formal corridor. Although thrilled at the thought of seeing my mother, I was frightened in case we confronted matron's stern face but her hard exterior melted into a warm welcome each time we set foot in the place.

I'd always find my mother tucked up in bed between white starched sheets, her alabaster face lighting up as I sprinted the last few yards to greet her. We stayed clenched in that special warm cuddle I missed last thing at night, chatting, she with pride in her voice wanting to know about my school exploits, how many gold stars for my times tables and the Afrikaans lessons I excelled in, me wanting to know why she was in there and how soon she would be home. Without her, life was unbearable, and I began to crave everything I had taken for granted. Apart from sitting next to her with her hand gripped firmly in mine, the other highlight of my visit was to accompany the nurse on her evening rounds; to be allowed to push the squeaking beverage trolley from ward to ward to serve the patients their last comforting cuppa of the day was a novel experience.

As to why my mother was in there, I was never sure. What I did know was that Connie was no substitute; I refused to let her comb my hair or to check that I had done my homework. I could not allow her to become my surrogate mother. The person I yearned for was my real mother and I could not wait for her to get out of that horrible place.

I tried to be brave each time we said our goodbyes with the reassurance from my father that she would be much better once she returned home. It comforted me and I believed him.

'And when she does, mind you don't play her up,' he would warn, wagging his finger.

Play her up? That was not something I did. My mother had patience by the bucket load. I was a good girl and, as far as I could tell, no bother to anyone. The occasions when I 'played her up' as my father put it must have been when as a young child we'd sit together at a circular glass-topped coffee table in the lounge, and she demonstrated the concept of arithmetic with some Cadbury's dummy chocolates used in window displays. 'Now there are eight chocolates. If I eat three of them, how many are left?' I loathed these sessions and guessed that was what my father must have been referring to.

The other incident happened when I had been playing next door with my friend Shirley. When my mother called that it was time to come in, I stuck my tongue out at her. I knew I had done something that displeased her when two extended arms reached over the three-foot barbed wire fence and, resembling a mechanical digger, she hauled me up into the air and over, with the sharpest of warnings never to do that again. I had no idea it was a shocking thing to do to a grownup, or anyone else for that matter.

Soon after that terrible scene I must have added to my mother's despair when one bath time, I flung her an innocent question.

'Are you my mum?'

She swung round. 'What makes you ask that?'

'Pamela wanted to know when I was playing round her house.' My mother's glaring eyes told me I should never have enquired.

'Look!' And to prove her point she yanked up her top to reveal the faded stretch marks. I often relive the pain of that question.

Shortly after her ordeal in hospital, in April 1957, my mother wrote to her sister, Linda:

> 'I have had a nasty time with my nerves again – it's nervous tension really – but I am glad to say I have put on two pounds of the five I lost. My friends and neighbours all say I'm looking much better now, more like my old self again. I

got Mrs Dodd [a neighbour] to write to Mother a few times because I was unable to do so. If Mother is with you don't read this to her because I haven't told her. I don't want her to worry. I was in bed for a few weeks before Xmas and went into Nursing Home on Boxing Day for nearly 3 weeks. They gave me shock treatment again to relax me, so of course I couldn't write, for as you know, it affects one's memory. I wasn't able to go out much for about 16 weeks. I felt dreadful and very weak from being in bed.'

The one thing that always made me cringe was to see my mother consume a mixture of raw beaten egg to which she would add a dash of brandy.

'It's to build up my strength,' she explained. It looked revolting and with my encouraging arm around her shoulders I'd watch the performance through slit fingers; somehow it helped with the agony of seeing her heave as it hit the back of her throat.

Desperate to return to England for a holiday she continued:

'I don't know when I shall be coming to England, but I would love to see you all again. Unfortunately, Vic has just paid out nearly £100 for specialist's fees that would have more than paid the fare one way. Vic says if I come over, I can't bring Diane because of her schooling being upset. It's such a problem. She is growing and quite a big girl now. On Saturday we went into town to see the University Student's Rag. It was very good and well worth seeing, but the noise didn't do my head much good. I still get awful pains in my head and I find I tire easily so I usually go to bed early and read. I eat quite well and don't worry about things as much as I used to. I really don't know whether the conditions at home cause me to have nerves or not but it's not a normal existence.
No more space.
Much love Blanche. Xx Write soon.'

The next few months passed in a blur. The fact I was now eight, my father informed me I could refer to our guest as Connie. I thought it was wonderful and felt grown up, but I was beginning to realize this aunt of mine was a mystery. I knew most of my relatives by name and that they lived in England, apart from my father's sister, Nancy, and her family who lived close by and Billy, my father's younger brother who had settled in Rhodesia (now Zimbabwe), but because I had never heard Connie's name mentioned as one of my relations, in my head I began to question her identity.

Although my mother had received treatment for her nerves, it was obvious she was buckling under the strain. In many ways, ours was an ordinary home but behind closed doors it was anything but ordinary. One-minute my parents appeared contented and then, for no visible reason, the atmosphere would change. My mother was no match for my head-strong father; no doubt wishing she had a tougher constitution to stand up to him. By remaining silent, she found a way to cope and, like a bird sitting on a nest, her determination to protect me was unbreakable; even in her darkest moments she showered me with her rock-hard, dependable love, never losing her temper or raising her voice. Every word that came out of her mouth was a caring word and a stabilizing influence I had come to rely on. That's how it was back then; by marrying my father she'd made her choice and was sticking to it.

I remember the day Connie returned after a visit to England to see her sister and she presented me with a life-size boy doll; I was playing in the front garden when my father opened the boot of his car and lifted out a cardboard box that was as tall as I was. I prised him from his layers of protective wrapping and christened him Roddy. Dressed in a two-piece of palest blue his vinyl head had a permanent smile and moveable eyes that followed me everywhere and from then on Roddy became my brother. At last I had a sibling to talk to. It wasn't until years later, when I reflected on Connie's holiday, that I realized what an enormous relief it must have been for my mother to have her out of the house. I wondered if the same could be said for my father.

If I wasn't entertaining myself in my make-believe world or lost in the adventures of my books, I revelled in the company of my friend Renee two doors away. Pretty faced with delicate chestnut curls and a nature to match, she too was an only child.

Her placid father specialised in exotic orchids and it was here in their back garden where we spent much of our time in his enormous greenhouses admiring and sketching those we thought were the most beautiful of the delicate blooms. Like Connie, Renee's mother was one of those rare women who, back in the 1950s, went out to work; it was in fashion, I seem to recall, and with her tall, trim figure, she was always elegant. Wary of her fierce nature, Renee and I would have our ears attuned to her purposeful high heeled clip clops as she approached for home at the end of the day, a sound that sent us scurrying to tidy up. And the day I made my exit and saw a black widow spider sunning itself in the letter box on their front gate left me in no doubt how fast I could sprint.

An unforgettable experience was when Renee had been riding my Triang tricycle in our back garden; with my over zealousness I pushed her and to my horror with a thud she fell backwards on the ground. I wondered what my fate would be as she lay on the ground motionless and without colour. It did not look good as my father scooped her up and drove her to hospital. That evening after she returned home with her arm in plaster, he asked me to deliver one of his parcels of chocolate tied in brown paper.

It was while playing with Renee that our doctors and nurses sessions took on a whole new meaning. We had been patching up our teddies and dolls with cuts and grazes until it was our turn to be the patient. That was when I returned home with Nivea cream applied to parts of my body where the manufacturers had never intended. 'Don't ever do that again!' came a stern finger-wagging warning from my mother.

Always a highlight was to listen out for the jovial ice cream vendors who peddled their tricycles with a gigantic square freezer unit attached to the back. With their white overalls a sharp contrast against their shiny jet-black skins, they would ring a hand bell to alert us of their presence. Clutching my pennies, Connie and I would have a race to see who was first in the queue for a tub of Lyons Maid ice cream or fruity frozen sucker, the equivalent of our British ice lollies.

During my time in Claremont, repeated bouts of asthma had begun to take their toll. Any exertion had me resting on my bed gasping for air. To ease my crippling breathlessness, my father would light a special vapour lamp and I'd dissolve multi-coloured tablets under my tongue. After months of suffering, he decided to seek the advice of a faith healer. I was never aware he was a believer but his effort to find a solution for my debilitating problem must have been a last resort.

The appointment was on a Saturday as my mother said she would not have to write a letter to request time off school. My father explained that he was taking me to see a gentleman who would fix my asthma. I named him Mr Fixit. While I waited, like Goldilocks I evaluated the leather chairs arranged round the perimeter of a dingy waiting room. I wondered what my fate would be, what this 'Mr Fixit' might say and what he might do to me. I was apprehensive but tried to hide my fear because I remembered the episode of my smallpox injection.

When the door opened, I was surprised to see an ancient gentleman with a stomach that hung over his trousers. He shook my father's hand and then mine with so much force I thought he might break it. An old desk separated us and the leather on his chair creaked as he lowered his hefty frame. And then he leant forward on his elbows and scrutinised me through rimless glasses perched on the end of his wrinkly nose. A discussion took place, about what I've no idea, except to hear him tell my father to refrain from giving me red meat for the next few weeks.

What followed was a miracle. Whether it was the abstention from red meat or sheer coincidence, thankfully I began to improve.

An unforgettable incident happened one boiling hot afternoon. My father had decided to paint the front of our house. With the can balanced precariously on top of his ladders, he had given me strict instructions. 'Just keep clear.' However, in my exuberance, the container fell to the ground with a sickening crash. I froze as a sea of pale rose-tinted liquid oozed along the concrete path. I ran indoors to explain. 'Sorry Dad. Sorry.' My father quivered with rage. I tried to dodge out of his arm's reach but was too slow. He landed a blow so powerful that I lost my balance and tumbled to the floor. The burning hot welts on my buttocks sent my mother rushing for her sugared water, a magic remedy that was almost worse than the beating. I can still taste that disgusting mixture. And then there was another occasion when the revolting concoction came my way. I'd invited friends to play in our back garden but in high spirits, Patrick took a swipe at a football and broke a window in our conservatory that sent an explosion of shattered glass in all directions. Everyone raced home not wishing to experience my father's wrath. Unfortunately for me, it was a while before they dared to return.

Whenever it was time for social gatherings or office functions my mother never accompanied my father alone; Connie was always in tow. Looking back into that scenario, one wonders what my father's employees must have thought and how my family was the source of gossip, the boss bringing his wife accompanied by another female friend. I cannot imagine how my mother tolerated the humiliation.

Apart from my visits with my mother to the hidden gem of Franschhoek, holidays were not something my father considered necessary; with an idyllic climate and sandy coves on the doorstep he would tell us that every day was like a holiday. But then something wonderful happened. The click of the latch on the front gate signalled his return from work. I did my customary dash to greet him. With a gigantic grin he scooped me into the air and carried me indoors.

'I've got something to tell you,' he said, kissing me on the cheek. 'You're going to love it.'

'Go on Dad. What is it?'

'Well; we're going on a holiday.'

'Yippee. Where? When?'

'I thought we'd have a camping adventure.'

'Camping?'

He nodded. 'It's a place called Onrus. It's surrounded by the Cape Overberg mountains with a beach and a lagoon nearby. Only a couple of hours drive from here.'

My mother glowed with anticipation and I thought my heart would leap out of my chest with excitement; it wasn't just because of the holiday but it was the fact it would be my first trip away with my parents. I ran and hugged my father.

'Wish we could go now.' I wore a permanent grin on my face and thought the day would never arrive; to sleep under canvas beneath a star-studded sky sent my heart racing. But as our expedition loomed, just before bed one evening I peered round

Connie's bedroom door and saw her packing her case. 'Where are you off to?' When I made my discovery that she would be joining us, I stomped off to my bedroom, kicked the door shut and howled into my pillow.

'Why, Mum?' I asked the following day. 'Why's she coming? It's not fair.'

'Go out and play,' she said, as though trying to ignore my repeated questioning. She must have been asking herself the same thing.

My father appeared upbeat about our imminent adventure although, for me, it was impossible to hide my disappointment.

'Will you stop pouting. Just be grateful,' he said. 'We'll leave at dawn. Need to make the most of our time.'

So, the following weekend, before the early morning sunshine had painted the sky blue, we were travelling up country through spectacular open landscape. It was like being in the middle of nowhere.

After a hot and dusty journey my father spied an idyllic spot to pitch our hefty army-style tent but to access it was down a steep embankment amongst a circle of shady trees. My cautious mother tried to warn him that it was a foolish idea.

'Never going to get back up,' she muttered. As usual, Connie took the situation in her stride and said nothing.

'Are you sure it's wise, Vic?' my mother asked again, but this time in a louder voice.

'Look! Will you stop keeping on. If you can get in, you can get out.'

Her pleading was to no avail. With his usual confidence my father negotiated the track, jamming on his brakes as we slid the last few yards to our destination.

With our tent pitched, pegs hammered into parched ground, guy ropes tightened, and camp beds erected, my father went in search of water so the adults could indulge in a thirst-quenching cuppa, courtesy of the primus stove. As early morning dawned, I sat on my stool outside the tent in awe of the fiery pinkish red hues and the stillness of the forest landscape interrupted only by the occasional flock of birds gliding as free souls.

I recall dipping in the balmy lagoon which offered a welcome reprieve from the blistering sun and watching, fascinated, as the moonlight shimmered like silver on the lifeless surface. And each evening, as darkness fell, my father lit the hissing hurricane lamps. I loved the intense smell of paraffin but what I loved even more were the fascinating shapes he made with his hands and the eerie elongated shadows it cast on the pitch-black canvas walls. Before going to bed, we gathered round a crackling campfire and in the glowing embers cooked thick slices of bread on toasting forks while my father told stories. He went into detail about camping as a boy scout when they decided to make sausage rolls to serve to the nuns. He had difficulty recounting the story for laughter, but they had collected freshly deposited horse manure and added a sprinkling to the meat. The nuns said they were the best flavoured sausage rolls they had ever tasted. It was obvious he had a roguish nature back in those days. While we cleared away, he would initiate the singing with his repertoire of army favourites, 'Come to the cookhouse door boys, come to the cookhouse door.' It was magical, listening to our voices echo through the quietness of the starry night.

With an axe clutched in his hand the collection of wood for those evening campfires had become a daily ritual for my father, while my daily jaunt was to wander along the dusty track to the nearby rondavel, a tiny straw roofed hut selling ice creams and drinks. On the other side of the counter, a short, wrinkled man with hardly any neck always made me giggle when he referred to me as the girl with the dark glasses and the freckly nose.

As our fun week neared an end, speculation began to grow as to how my father would achieve the ascent up the steep incline. He tried to duck the issue by assuring us it would not be a problem. With the tent and camping equipment crammed into the boot of the car, it was a tense time as we watched his efforts from a distance. Amid noisy revving, wheels spinning, a pungent smell of burning, and clouds of swirling grit, and a little less rubber on the tyres, he stood back and scratched his head.

'Told you!' I said'

'Will you be quiet,' he warned.

'Oh, Vic!' came from Connie and I think my mother thought we would be there forever. With a calm confidence, my father decided that making the car lighter would do the trick, so he hauled the camping gear onto the arid bushes at the side of the sandy track. Muttering under his breath and shouting words I had never heard before, he made another attempt. Making little headway, he conceded and went off to rustle up the assistance of four muscular, sun-tanned locals who conversed in Afrikaans. With pushing from behind and rope pulling from the front the car inched its way up the sharp gradient.

'Phew,' my father said, extracting a hanky from his shorts pocket to dab his dripping brow. 'Lucky it wasn't any steeper.' I sensed relief on his face knowing he was bringing the car back with us and his keenness to prove a point that where there's a will, there's a way. Everyone laughed during the journey home.

Soon after that unforgettable holiday I returned home from school one day and heard the word 'move'.

CHAPTER 8
ON THE MOVE

Why and where would this move be taking us? With my father's social aspirations, he explained his wish to have another bungalow built and within weeks had snapped up a suitable plot in Newlands on the gentle slopes of Table Mountain, an affluent area renowned today for its rugby and cricket grounds.

Daily discussions took place as to the style of our new property and at weekends we piled into my father's car and headed off to nearby Bishopscourt and Constantia with their enviable residences and long sweeping drives a measure of their prosperity. Feasting his eyes on their architectural splendour, he cruised along the tree-lined avenues with me ducked down in the back of the car from embarrassment but the height of my awkwardness was when he turned off the engine to sketch any features that he considered desirable.

To clear the land from dense undergrowth, towering pines, and the odd snake or two, my father mustered together an army of burly blokes. With skin like oiled ebony and noses as wide as their smile, they were always laughing. At weekends, he crammed his zealous workforce with their bulging biceps into his grey Ford Zephyr (six cylinders, he'd always remind us), while the night before, to satisfy their insatiable appetites, my mother and I prepared mountainous stacks of cheese and tomato sandwiches which we wrapped in brown greaseproof paper. Because the overpowering stench from their stale sweat made me choke, the most important task was to ensure we left the car windows wound down overnight.

To witness my mother and Connie studying the architect's plans laid out on the dining room table was nothing unusual but to hear Connie talk about 'when we move', it was obvious she would be joining us. She had been living with us for the best part of seven years and I was beginning to think it might make a refreshing change to be a family of three again. It was impossible to remember what life had been like before her arrival, but I was aware that we did not have the unrest that had so often become the pattern of our everyday lives.

With planning permission granted, building began in earnest and after the topping out ceremony, Umgwemla, our cheery night watchman, made our garage his make-shift home for the following few months. As I endeavoured to teach him English, he in return demonstrated how to make the fascinating click sound in his Xhosa language but what mesmerised me was to watch him clean his perfect pearly teeth with a simple piece of twig after his evening meal of maize.

With Bertha; Bunty, our Maltese poodle; Tinkles, my yellow budgerigar; and Timothy, Thomas, Oswald, Archibald, and Baby, my five tortoises eager to sample the delights of their new shrubbery, the day after my tenth birthday we graced Pinewood Road with our arrival. But it soon became apparent there were other inhabitants. Rain spiders, black, hairy, and enormous, would sometimes appear from nowhere and to wake up in the morning and discover one of these unwelcome visitors on my bedroom wall sent me screaming for my father's assistance.

'Dad! Quick! Get the broom.'

'They won't hurt you,' he assured me. Well, I wasn't going to chance it because, when I checked, it seemed they were partial to cockroaches, which wasn't a bad thing, and crickets which would have delighted my father, but I had also read they could inflict a defensive bite. But that was nothing compared to the mild hysteria we experienced early one summer's morning. With everyone still tucked up in their beds, my mother's first mission was to let Bunty into the garden but when she took a closer inspection and discovered a snake entwined around the hosepipe outside the back door she rushed for help. She loathed the sinister creatures and thereafter did her daily check for lurking reptiles. My father said it was a Cape Cobra. I merely took his word for it.

With a lot of thought and time invested, our bungalow was a design well ahead of its day. Expansive full length windows maximised the panoramic backdrop of Table Mountain, while the interior and exterior feature walling constructed from natural stone excavated out of the foundations added a touch of rugged grandeur and in our light and airy sitting room stylish red Cintique chairs together with a long low sofa covered in charcoal fabric reflected the colours in the wall to wall abstract curtaining.

Moving in day, February 1959

It soon became apparent that our arrival in this sophisticated neighbourhood caused intrigue; Connie's presence had not gone unnoticed.

'Gentleman in the house opposite wants to know if Connie's my sister.' I ran home and announced to my mother who was at the kitchen table weighing the ingredients for her rock cakes.

'Sister?'

She rolled her eyes and hurled the dried fruit into the mixture. With just three years between them, her anger was understandable.

'Do I look that old?' was all I kept hearing.

But my most significant memory soon after our arrival was when my father demanded he sleep on his own in the back bedroom; to be near his cloakroom, he told me, but that required my mother and Connie having to share the bedroom in the front. I thought it strange that my father opted not to sleep with my mother, but it was more than I dared to mention. Not only had Connie invaded my mother's home but the chilling invasion of her privacy must have pushed my mother to her limits; she must have wondered if it was the end of her marriage. For me, life was confusing. I never knew what he would insist on next. Sometimes I think back to those days, questioning how my father could have expected his wife to agree to his demands.

With school friends living in the same road and our mothers not driving, my father got involved in a lift sharing scheme. If I were playing netball on the days when it was his turn to do the school run, he would park the car opposite the court in order to observe the game. I hoped I had done him proud with my efforts, but there was always a post-mortem afterwards. He was my harshest critic. 'Need to be more assertive and tackle.'

Away from the confines of home, days were long and idyllic. To wander barefoot on sizzling pavements was bliss; I recall one summer they were so fiendishly hot there had been reports of frying an egg. Pleasures were simple; whether we were riding our bikes, playing outdoor games or gathering wild proteas by the armful, we were free to roam; and to avoid the trauma of home-life I invented any excuse to stay out for as long as possible. With a tennis court in their grounds, we practised our game courtesy of the Lees family, but it was their neighbours who became the envy of the street. The discovery that Tessa Gage's parents had a swimming pool took my outdoor pursuits to new heights. With their laid-back approach, an army of us would make use of the facilities, sometimes rising at an unearthly hour to maximise our fun, even during the winter months when it deluged.

During my time in Newlands I became friendly with the Roup family. They lived opposite and had two sons, Herman and Julian but it was their daughter, Janine, who was my real buddy. Their father owned Enterprise Bakeries, suppliers of bread, cake, and biscuits to the Cape and it was here that I had a terrifying experience with the family's pet pony. It was my first time in the saddle, the pair of us slowly trotting and then without warning we took off, the frivolous equine half bolting, half charging, but an ordeal soon forgotten when we entered the factory and breathed in the comforting and addictive sweet-smelling aroma of baking and to select from the long tiered cooling racks what delicacies took our fancy is something I will never forget.

Diane off to Bloubergstrand for a holiday, 1960

Not only that, but half an hour's drive outside Cape Town, at a place called Bloubergstrand, the Roups had a holiday home on the shimmering Atlantic seashore, where shells were plentiful, and the rhythmic sound of the ocean lapped at our feet. And with an invitation to join them for the occasional weekend, their friendly driver collected me in their mother's black and white Karmann Ghia sports car. I was never happier than when I was in Janine's company; those welcome breaks allowed me to push to the back of my mind the days sometimes shrouded in uncertainty.

Diane Harding

Christmases in Cape Town were sweltering and sunny and fell in the middle of the long school holidays. Gardens were a spectacle with voluptuous hydrangeas and red-hot pokers and when my father ordered a delivery of festive drinks, as a special treat he would add a dozen bottles of fizzy raspberry to the list. With Connie's flamboyant nature, every year without fail she headed her Christmas list with first a yacht, followed by a mink coat and then a Jaguar, always in that order. Father Christmas never did fulfil her grandiose wishes, but it became a constant source of amusement.

It was the lounge that held our lives together; where we relaxed as though we were the perfect family, me playing with my dolls, the adults reading the *Cape Argus* newspaper, (my father swore the Saturday edition gave him a throbbing headache and to see him with a vinegar bandage tied round his head was like a scene from Jack and Jill), listening to the gramophone or gathered round the radio for entertainment; it was a crucial part of everyday life. *In Town Tonight* was one such programme with local businesspeople interviewed and interspersed with records of their choosing. When my father received an invitation to make a guest appearance, for weeks beforehand he agonised over the music he should request; it wasn't his thing, nor my mother's, apart from her rendition of Pat Boon's *Blue Moon*. But he was a massive fan of Mario Lanza so that was a definite. As for the other records, that's where Connie came to the rescue with her vast knowledge.

One of my school friends, Eileen Whiting, lived in a bungalow nearby where suburbia met the gateway to the mountainous forest. With a nervous disposition like me, she, too, was an only child. To go to our respective houses for sleepovers was a novelty and when it was bath-time, we requested our mothers to play tokoloshe (from Zulu mythology) by ramming the hosepipe through the bathroom window and pretending to terrify us. Both sets of parents had struck up a close friendship, but my biggest thrill was accompanying them to the drive-in cinema. As night fell, Eileen and I would don our pyjamas, grab a blanket and bundle into the back of her parents' grey Wolsey (I think it was). The impressive outdoor movie screen was in a gigantic parking area, each allotted space with a concession stand and a speaker her father positioned inside on the dashboard. To order drinks and snacks and have them delivered to the car added to the adventure.

Mealtimes in our home were a formal affair; laid with a silver cruet set, bone-handled cutlery and cloth napkins rolled into their silver serviette rings to differentiate ownership, we ate off Midwinter's 'Zambesi' china. Because my father was a fussy individual, my mother and I would sit at the dinner table on hyperalert; it had become a perpetual battle ground, with scenes triggered all too often over trivialities. I have no idea what my mother had prepared for dinner on this one occasion but whatever it was, his ranting caused her to leap from the table saying she felt peculiar. Pounding to her bedroom with me in hot pursuit had become a regular occurrence but I could never understand why Connie showed no concern and merely continued with her meal. Whenever these unpleasant eruptions occurred, my mother complained of pains in her head and feeling paralysed down her left side.

'You don't think I've had a stroke, do you?'

'Poppycock,' would be my father's response.

Deeply sensitive to her plight, I would coax her back to calmness until she felt it safe to venture back out. It was after one of these scenes that I caught her perched on the edge of the bath with a cigarette clutched in her shaking hand. That was the first time I had witnessed her smoking. 'Need something to calm my nerves,' she said, rubbing her forehead as she exhaled. 'Otherwise I might go mad.' I knew she had hit rock bottom whenever she dropped her composure in front of me, but it seemed there was little I could do to help.

I try hard to forget the days when, as a young child, I'd sit on my bed figuring out what was happening around me and even now, when I least expect it, strong memories come hurtling back.

My father always demonstrated high morals. Soon after moving to Newlands, I was forbidden to play with the neighbour's little boy because he'd spied him urinating through our wire fence into his cherished dahlia border and there was another occasion when he heard a mild swear word from little Zach so that meant no contact either.

These were trivialities compared to the time when Bertha announced she was getting married. My father invited her fiancé to our house and saw it his duty to deliver a harsh lecture on the rights and wrongs in a marriage, discussing with him how to care for his future wife and the bitter consequences of straying. I sometimes think back to those days and wonder what scenarios Bertha might have conjured up knowing Connie lived with us.

My father was a man of extremes; if he wasn't angry, he was acting the fool. Fuelled by a determination to achieve, he was shrewd and persuasive. Although he drove me mad at times, with his awkward ways and fiery temper, he was not one to indulge in drinking or swearing and was faultless for his endless energy. If a job's worth doing, it's worth doing well, was his motto. Although some families employed black gardeners, sometimes more if the property stood in sizeable grounds, it was my father who tended ours. With his muscular tanned legs, he toiled like a machine bare-chested from sunrise to sunset to landscape our back garden. With his keen eye, nothing was ever out of place and if anything needed supporting, his sticks stood upright like soldiers. Gigantic beef tomatoes formed a crimson backdrop in his manicured borders and when they were ripe, I had permission to fill my oval wicker basket. Even now, that pungent aroma of freshly picked tomatoes has my senses rushing back to my childhood. Using his lathe, woodwork was his self-taught hobby. If it was wooden, we had it and to venture into the garage and inhale the fresh sawdust was addictive.

Victor in the front garden at Newlands watering his prized dahlias

During my time in Newlands, I had acquired an autograph book. Covered in grey velvet, I had requested my friends to sign it; some had compiled little poems, a few had printed rhymes and others had added jokes. One or two had even sketched pictures. But on the middle page, I had printed the headings 'the family' and underneath 'the household'. I was intrigued to see that Connie had signed her name under 'the family'. It must have dawned on me that, although I referred to her as an 'aunt', she was not a true family member.

I struggled to understand my father's erratic behaviour. As no two days were ever the same, it was little wonder my mother fantasised about visiting relatives back in England. It was a conversation she would often engage in, but my father had made it quite clear he would not allow me to accompany her, as he said it would impact on my schooling. Not that it had any meaning back then, but he would sometimes remind me just how expensive my education was, although, as far as I could tell, money was never an issue. We enjoyed a comfortable lifestyle; the minute transistor radios were in the shops, he walked up the garden path after work one evening with the invention blaring out music.

I dreaded overhearing my mother talk about her family and her longing to see them and when one of these visits began to gather momentum, fear gripped me on a monstrous scale.

'Please, Mum, don't go. Don't leave me.' I begged every night before bed. I asked her why it was so important.

'Haven't seen my sisters for years,' she tried to explain. 'Besides, I could do with a break.'

'Can't they come over to us?' The thought of her leaving caused nightmares. It was bad enough when she had gone into hospital when I was eight and I did not relish going through that same agony ever again.

'It won't be for long.' But that was of little consolation, knowing she would be gone for months. I had no idea how I would cope without her by my side; she was the only person I turned to for comfort and reassurance.

'I'll miss you terribly, but I promise to send lots of post cards.'

'Wish I could come with you.' It was all I could talk about and as the reality of her leaving hit home, I cried on and off for days.

When the time came to say our farewells, with a heavy heart I hugged her goodbye, leaving me to speculate when she would be returning. Looking back, I could understand her desperation to get away and how leaving me behind must have torn her apart.

She wrote regularly, telling me how she loved me and was missing me and whenever a card fell through the letterbox, seeing her handwriting made me feel connected to her. Although I had made a chart so I could cross off the days until her return, it was a disconcerting time. My mother took all my affection. Having Connie in the house was no substitute for her generosity of spirit and I prayed she would never disappear again.

Another poignant memory while living in Newlands was my eleventh birthday party. My mother's sewing machine whirred late into the night to create a dress in lemon chiffon with the stitching of the hem assigned to Connie minutes before the first guest was due to arrive. I had invited school friends and those local, although it was touch and go whether Kerrith MacKenzie would make it. Laid low with a stomach bug, his parents did not think it advisable but after repeated pestering they gave him the go ahead. But it soon became clear that he had not made a full recovery; with the party games in full swing he vomited at various stations in the back garden.

'Knew he shouldn't have come,' my father announced, as he followed him around to cover the evidence with shovelfuls of sand. Apart from that mishap, it was my most memorable birthday ever.

After the success of my fete in Claremont, when I'd borrowed John Dodd's wind-up record player and *The Laughing Policeman* played non-stop, I thought it would be an excellent idea to hold another event, again in aid of Dr Barnardo's. I wrote persuasive letters to various businesses who generously donated soft drinks and sweets for the various stalls and, with my father's endless supply of chocolate, there were prizes for all the activities. During the week, my mother's baking for the cake stall sent a mouth-watering aroma wafting through the house and my father entered in the spirit of things too. His 'Spin the Wheel' was an impressive construction and he even rigged up a stall to come and see the 'Man-Eating Fish', which, of course, was my father sat at a table eating fish! It was only a penny to enter but I always hoped the children did not think they'd been short changed. In our back garden, *Little Yellow Polka Dot Bikini* belted out from the record player and the lucky dip, with sawdust courtesy of my father's woodwork projects, proved popular with everyone.

The freedom was what I loved best about my time in Newlands but when I was twelve, I stopped in my tracks one day when my father used a four-letter word. It was a word I had heard before.

Diane Harding

CHAPTER 9
GOODBYE CAPE TOWN

The last time my father mentioned the word 'move' was two years before when we were leaving Claremont. And now it had reared its horrid head again. I had heard discussions about the political unrest, even mention of my parents returning to England, so perhaps that was the reason.

It was not speculation. My fabulous home was up for sale and I was leaving Newlands. It didn't seem long ago I was drowning in my tears when my mother left for England and once more, I was back on my pillow sobbing.

Knowing that my father's artistic eye was in every piece of natural stone he had painstakingly selected from the foundations, he admitted that it was going to be a wrench but he tried to soften the blow by explaining that we would be staying in the Alameda Hotel while he organised a transfer back with Cadbury's. Even my mother had a renewed spring in her step; I often wondered if it was the thought of returning to be nearer her relatives that kept her going.

'A hotel? Are we really?'

Dad beamed and nodded. Well that sounded different. I had never spent a night in a hotel, let alone lived in one but first I had to adjust to the fact I would again be bidding my friends farewell; I was the last to arrive in the neighbourhood and the first to leave. The one small consolation was that the Alameda would be nearer my school so no lift sharing would be necessary; I would be able to ride my bicycle there and back each day.

Bidding Bertha farewell saddened us; we had all grown fond of one another. With everyone deep in their thoughts, my father drove her back to her shanty town existence with its makeshift corrugated dwellings and the most basic of necessities. As we bumped our way down a rutted track, I saw shirtless children playing with metal hoops and scrawny chickens pecking in the dirt, a sharp contrast to what she had left behind. Laden with items we were unable to take with us, Bertha also promised to look after Tinkles, my budgie. Thank goodness the hotel permitted dogs.

When I heard Connie was off on an extended holiday to the Lebanon I leapt for joy; things were beginning to look promising. I also learnt that I would be sharing a bedroom with my parents for the duration of our stay and sighed with relief at the prospect of having them to myself. Perhaps moving would have its advantages.

That was until one sultry day, fatigued from the humidity, the three of us decided to have a nap. I had never witnessed any outward affection between my parents, never a kiss hello or a kiss goodbye and certainly never any holding of hands but on this sweltering afternoon I observed something startling. They had separate beds, there was nothing unusual with that, but with my father thinking I was asleep from the corner of my eye I noticed he had sidled into my mother's bed. I heard movement and the rustling of bedclothes. I lay there, stuck to the sheets, unable to move a limb. As the perspiration dripped from me, I wondered what might be going on.

The next thing I knew I woke for dinner.

Our meals in the dining room were a relaxing affair; my father was on his best behaviour and to have Darnie, our waiter, serve us at table was a novelty. However, my mother never fancied her cornflakes after she spied him scooping the cereal out of the box and into her bowl with his bare hands. 'Goodness knows where they've been,' followed by 'hope he's washed them,' was her mantra every morning thereafter.

It was a happy time for us all; my father had taken to whistling and my mother's deep furrows had vanished.

After six months at the Alameda and no sign of our departure for England, the farewells I had imagined were unfounded. Since the offer of a position with Cadbury's had not materialised, for the next twelve months my father decided to rent a flat at Herschel Gardens. When was all this moving to end?

Because our apartment was a temporary move, my father explained that we would be able to manage with the two bedrooms it offered. The only positive was that the block of flats was opposite my school and I would now be able to walk.

I was now thirteen and this was to be my fourth address. With little freedom in the hotel, I viewed this short-term abode with more enthusiasm and having tasted what it was like to be alone with my parents, I looked forward to it continuing.

Our wooden crates arrived out of storage but with every piece of furniture sold when we left Newlands, my father purchased the necessary items to tide us over, only this time they were second hand. The gigantic warehouse had a vast choice; once more it was individual beds for my parents and two singles for my room, but the teak dressing table for my parents' bedroom held my attention. It had three drawers, the middle one still crammed with makeup of every description. I was in my element experimenting, including a cooling stick of camphor which I had mistaken for deodorant; my underarms burned for days.

I wondered why the need for two beds in my cramped room, but I soon had my answer; Connie had returned from her holiday and would be sharing my bedroom. It was now my turn to have her invade my privacy. I did not dare make my feelings known, but I could have cried. With one small wardrobe between us, we each had two shelves but, given that she possessed more clothes than me, it left little space for mine. It seemed Connie could not keep away from my home; I could never understand the attraction, although I had come to realize that it was always my mother objecting to her presence and never my father.

Although in hot climates cockroaches are common, with the discovery that we had an infestation my father never did things by halves and sprinkled the insect powder liberally. Unfortunately, Bunty had taken a liking to it with atrocious consequences. With my father heaving, Connie out and my mother on her bed with one of her peculiar bouts, it fell upon me to clean up a sea of odorous mess. The only consolation was that it was on the floorboards and not the carpet.

My father's showing off at mealtimes had returned and knowing what to say, or what not to say, was a matter of judgement. Even before my mother had taken her place at the table, she'd be wringing her hands in anticipation of his outbursts. I knew she was not sleeping well and had been to the doctor, but her trips for reassurance were nothing new. With the suggestion that she try walking for relaxation, we'd take ourselves off to the nearby botanical gardens where she instilled in me an acute awareness of nature's wonders and to appreciate the beauty and sights of everyday life: butterflies with their fragile wings; the flora and fauna around us; and the striking sunsets. And then on our return to the flat she would remove the hairpins from her bun so I could comb her long dark locks. These outings had become routine, but I found it strange that my father and Connie chose not to accompany us.

During my time at Herschel, I had become firm friends with Jenny Saker, slender and pretty with wavy russet, shoulder length hair that matched her eyes. Living in Kenilworth, we were now much closer to one another and, with her brother, Martin, and mother, Anita, she often extended a warm invitation for me to join them. With her outsize kindliness, Mrs Saker became a second mother to me, frequently driving us girls in her trusted sage green Fiat to choose dress material and then assisting us in the making of our garments. Jenny and I became inseparable and, apart from our midnight feasts, if I stayed over with her family at weekends, I'd accompany them to the Vineyards hotel in Newlands, where the firm favourite for lunch was always Wiener Schnitzel. We also joined the local tennis club, playing in weekend matches and almost fried on the gravel courts in the summer of 1963 when the scorching temperature reached record levels.

Jenny's mother took me under her wing. I saw my mother in Anita's thoughtfulness; she I know was grateful to her for affording me the opportunity to have a break from Connie's continual presence. Although the real reason for my unorthodox home life had escaped me, it was obvious it had not escaped her.

Even as a young teenager, I could never understand why the situation in our house was so troublesome. Now, I can hardly believe I did not figure it out.

At last I discovered the date when we would be leaving for England. It was 31 May 1963. Apart from being a public holiday for Independence Day, it was also my father's forty-fifth birthday.

An impatient fourteen-year-old had waited restlessly for the momentous day to arrive and, as I ticked off the days in my head, my feelings swung between sadness and joy; sadness having to bid farewell to the place I called home and joy at the thought of sharing a cabin with my parents. I focussed on that aspect more than anything. Looking back, I think it was this that gave me the greatest thrill.

Once again, with wooden crates packed to capacity, I watched as my father nailed the lids and stuck labels on saying 'ENGLAND'. Seeing our destination printed in bold letters told me that, like it or not, our departure was imminent.

Before we sailed, two touching letters dropped through our letterbox. One was from Bertha, the other from Martin Gwayi, who had been instrumental in helping clear the thick undergrowth from our plot in Newlands.

Bertha wrote:

> 'Dear Master, Madam, Miss Connie, Diane,
> I hereby wish all of you a happy and pleasant sea voyage and also prosperity in England.
> I also take this opportunity to say how kind-hearted all of you have been to me in these past few years. I've never met any family so kind, loving, considerate and sincere as all of you has been that's why my heart is broken on your departure.
> Furthermore, thank you for everything. Although I'm thanking you somehow, I still feel I'm not thanking you enough.
> Please remember me, as I will always remember all of you.
> I remain yours,
> Bertha
> With Love. Xx'

It sickened me to read that the letter wished Connie a 'pleasant sea voyage'. To discover that she would be accompanying us back to England crushed my optimism. I could never understand why she followed us everywhere. All I could do was agonise for my poor mother. Martin's letter read:

'Dear Sir,
Let me write these few lines to you. I see that you are just about to leave this beautiful City of ours. Before your departure I want to express my views to you about our friendship.
Sir, I want to tell you that your absence here will be of a great loss. Your presence here, encouraged me too much in my horticultural work. Sir, I want to state that I am like a bereaved young fellow, because of your departure. By the use of the word departure, I mean to say that my companion who usually helped me in my garden work is leaving me.
Secondly, your departure will cause a great loss of a beautiful young flower which tossed its head when I waved my hand at it. The young flower is your housemaid who will not be seen by me because it may happen that she will get an employment at a far-off distance.
Mr/Mrs Berry, in my language there is what we say people who met each other before, shall meet each other in future. I hope that I will meet you overseas provided that the Africans get their passport from the Government of this country.
With best wishes and kind regards to you all.
Yours sincerely
Martin H Gwayi'

With an invitation to spend my final night with Jenny's family I couldn't have been happier, although Martin thought he would play one last trick; he apple-pied my bed which made it impossible to find a way between the sheets. I collapsed into tears. It was all too much.

The following morning, we were on our way by taxi to the 25,000 ton *Athlone Castle*, the mail boat that was to take us on our momentous voyage to England.

Up on deck my mother and I stood huddled at the railings.

Jenny and her family were at the quayside for the send-off and with a lump in my throat we hung on to our friendship clutching brightly coloured streamers.

The sun beamed down on us under a flawless soft blue sky, as though the elements had conspired to give us the perfect send-off and as our ship nudged from her moorings, with one last lurch, the ties with my homeland had severed. My eyes welled as I thought about the youth I was leaving behind. I glanced up at my mother and wondered what she might be thinking. She had a hanky in her hand, but I'm sure for her they were tears knowing she'd be seeing her family in two weeks and no doubt deep sorrow for shattered dreams.

I have no recollection of my father's reaction as he bid tot siens (Afrikaans for goodbye and a language my parents never did master) to his post war vision.

I waved my hand and took one last glance at the splendour of the shoreline. It was a massive wrench bidding farewell to the country I had known as home for the last fourteen years not knowing when, if ever, I would be returning. It was hard to imagine not having those spoilt-for-choice beaches and open-air lidos at my fingertips. I would miss the abundance of fresh fruit, guavas which I adored (sweaty armpits, my father said they smelled of).

As the iconic framework of Table Mountain faded into the distance, I watched my home slowly vanish. Although fuelled by an exhilaration for the unknown, I had underestimated how emotional my packing up and seeing things for the last time would be.

Every year during May I still think about the preparations to leave, the butterflies in my stomach and the click of the key when my father locked the empty flat for the final time.

I wondered what it would be like making new friends and beginning another school in a country I knew nothing about. The only certainty was that I would be seeing my grandma within hours of arriving. I liked the sound of that, as it was eleven years ago when she came over to Cape Town for a holiday.

As the ship cut its course into the notoriously rough Cape Rollers, within an hour my mother was flat on her bunk feeling nauseous, unsure whether it was the choppy sea, from cracking her head on an overhead steel girder soon after boarding or the sheer relief that, at long last, we were bound for England.

I laughed when I learnt that my father was sharing a cabin with a grotesque Greek who kept him awake at night with his snoring. My mother said it served him right. But cabin number 532 was where the three females slept for the next fourteen days. Small and confined, the only appealing aspect was the porthole which offered a view of the glistening silk ocean as darkness fell. When I asked Connie why she was leaving Cape Town, all she said was that she had decided it was time that she, too, returned to England. My biggest regret was not being able to share a cabin with my parents and I wondered if it ever occurred to her that I might have welcomed the chance to be alone with them on that momentous voyage. I still reflect about that lost opportunity.

By a strange coincidence Beverley Ellis, one of my school friends, was also on board with her parents, bound for a holiday in England, so, right from the start, I had company. Beverley's parents were intrigued to know who Connie was, although I feel sure Jenny's mother, a good friend of Mrs Ellis, must have explained.

The photograph I recently unearthed shows us in the dining room with our waiter standing nearby; it's heart-warming to see my mother beaming. Both she and Connie are studying me appearing coy. Had someone embarrassed me by making a comment? It was here on-board ship I had my first kiss. A lad had been eyeing me up and after following me to my cabin one evening he pinned me behind the door to perform the deed. It left me unimpressed: he had obviously eaten roast beef for dinner. After that encounter I made sure I avoided him at all costs.

From left Diane, Connie, Blanche and Victor in the dining room aboard the Athlone Castle, 1963

All I could do was fantasize about my new adventure and on the fourteenth of June, at 6am British time, we docked at Southampton.

Dizzy with excitement, I rolled out of my bunk for the final time and watched fearfully as a crane hoisted Bunty's kennel over the side of the ship into a waiting van to take him to Hampshire for his six months quarantine against rabies. Although it was mid-June, my thin cotton dress was inadequate; greeted with an ethereal mist that hung over the quayside like gossamer, the grey, damp chill of the morning clung to my body and nipped at my fingers.

Just as my parents had emigrated fifteen years earlier to make South Africa their castle, it was now my turn to make England mine. With no fixed abode, I felt overwhelmed, as though plucked from my roots, and dumped into alien surroundings.

I was intrigued to discover my 'family' of four was to split up, all of us heading off in separate directions; Connie was meeting up with friends in London, my father was travelling to his sister's in Bournemouth, my mother and I were catching a train to visit her elderly mother who now lived with Freda and Frank in Surrey and what items we were fortunate enough to bring with us were en route for storage, destination unknown.

Diane Harding

CHAPTER 10
HELLO ENGLAND

The time I had spent languishing over photographs in glossy magazines were finally put to the test. I marvelled at the unfolding landscape; the sight of picturesque hamlets and farmsteads with quaint, white-washed cottages nestled amidst rolling verdant hills, everything in sight a sharp contrast compared to the sun-scorched scrubland I had left behind.

With each mile we travelled, my excitement grew. As the motion of the steam train took us ever nearer to our destination, I was impatient to see my grandma who, apart from seeing her sniffing her smelling salts when I was a young child, was someone I could barely remember. I also had difficulty in remembering my cousins whom I had met decades earlier. Getting to know David would take a little longer as he was away at Cambridge University studying medicine, but I was able to renew a friendship with his younger brother, Peter, who with his six foot frame and wavy brown hair, at fifteen I found appealing.

With hugs and introductions out of the way, Grandma was quick to ascertain Connie's whereabouts; the fact she was accompanying us back to England had given cause for alarm. 'Finally,' my mother told her, 'she's buggered off.' I took note as my mother never resorted to swearing, although why I cannot imagine. Grandma threw her hands in the air and let out an audible sigh of relief. My mother beamed too. 'Yes.' She said crossing her fingers on both hands. 'It's a new life and a new beginning.' And, as she had already pointed out, we would at last be a family of three.

We had got rid of Connie and my father was in the south of England. Everything appeared idyllic; for the time being it was just me and my mother. When I think back to those days, she must have thought she was dreaming.

To maximise our time with Grandma, she had arranged for us to stay nearby with her long-standing friend, Mrs Acres, in her terraced, old-world country cottage overlooking Effingham Church, its spire poking out through heavy treetops, just enough for me to make out the hands on the clock face. We accessed upstairs via a narrow 'Alice in Wonderland' twisting staircase and in her gleaming white bathroom water to wash was from a geyser, a small device on the wall that provided hot water at the turn of a handle. To the rear of the cottage, her quaint bedroom window overlooked a profusion of sweet-smelling copper hollyhocks. This was the England I had envisaged; pigeons cooing, cows mooing and a village clock chiming on the quarter hour. I wrote to my friend Jenny (Wren, I'd nicknamed her) to tell her all about it.

Following our short stay in Surrey, for the next fortnight we joined my father at his sister's home in Bournemouth before heading up to Bromsgrove to visit my grandma's sister, Sarah, and her husband, Dick.

This was an experience I could never have imagined. Nestled amidst a row of terraced Victorian cottages, the house had a drab exterior. With no electricity, evening illumination was courtesy of candles and hissing gas mantles, tiny mesh lights lit with matches. Their kitchen was a scullery, a small area off the dining room with a sink and wooden draining board and a contraption in the corner I had never before clapped eyes on; it was a large metal container called a copper that stood on the floor and heated water for washing clothes. Worse still, there was no upstairs running water; instead, we filled a jug for our morning ablutions. I hated washing, as the icy water made me shiver. There was even a white china chamber pot under the bed, 'just in case', Aunt Sarah said, but there was no way I would be using that.

With the discovery that they had a primitive outside toilet, a wooden bench with a hole in it, I thought I would never again spend a penny. Were all houses like this or had I struck lucky staying in Mrs Acres' pretty cottage? Nothing could have prepared me. Everything was so different from the ultra-modern facilities I had grown up with.

On our first night, Sarah and Dick had made a huge sacrifice by insisting my mother and I use their bedroom. By means of a flickering candle, we groped our way up the narrow staircase and fumbled our way to the room. In the corner, the marble washstand glimmered and as we negotiated their elaborate iron-framed bedstead and sank our weary bodies into a lumpy feather mattress piled high with scratchy woollen blankets, each time we moved the coil springs creaked. With our hands clasped to our mouths we tried not to make our hysterics heard but from the adjoining room Uncle Dick banged on the wall wanting to know what the noise was about. After that sleepless night, my mother moved into the spare bedroom and I slept on the two-seater settee in their dingy front room. In the alcoves either side of the green tiled fireplace were shelves cluttered with souvenirs from seaside jaunts and a maroon chenille curtain pulled across the front door to keep out the draught. I always woke early on that sofa awaiting the clunk of the morning newspaper through the letterbox.

In the dining room, sitting at a scrubbed wooden table with a storage drawer at the end, Dick devoured his bowl of bread and milk each evening before retiring to bed. I had developed an aversion to milk from an early age and detested having to kiss him goodnight with soggy detritus adhered to his white moustache tinged ginger from heavy smoking.

Whenever possible, I took comfort loitering in their rear garden. Stocked with perfumed crimson and cream rose bushes there was a long concrete path that tracked down to a railway line at the far end. Here, steam trains passed through but to negotiate the Lickey Hills, the steepest incline in Britain, sometimes two or more engines were required to tackle the gradient. Whenever I heard a train approach, I would rush down with both arms waving to catch the attention of the passengers and engine drivers. Without fail, through a blanket of smoke and belching black smuts, people smiled and waved back. The sound of the whistle and the deafening noise from the pistons was like a scene from *The Railway Children*. Seeing those trains fascinated me and I was impatient for the next to pass by but, because of the Dickensian conditions, I prayed we would soon be moving on.

With so much hopping about from one county to another, I was beginning to understand the geography of England faster than I could ever have imagined. After happy goodbyes to Bromsgrove, our next stop was to see my auntie Linda and her husband, Jimmy, who lived in Formby, near Liverpool. By contrast, theirs was a stylish detached property in a leafy suburban area but, during our stay, the Profumo affair was in full swing, the scandal that made headlines on all television news bulletins. Every time I heard the sordid details about Christine Keeler's sexual involvement with the politician, I felt the colour rush to my cheeks. At fourteen, the mere mention of the word sex did not make for easy listening. My mother had never breathed a word to me about such matters; the nearest she got to an explanation was one evening when we lived in Newlands, she in the shower and me in the bath, with an announcement, 'You know it takes two, don't you?'

After our nomadic few weeks finally, it was time to move to a place of our own.

CHAPTER 11
A FAMILY OF THREE

C adbury's had now branched out into the cake market and my father had accepted a position at their Bournville headquarters in Birmingham.

After researching the area, he secured a ground floor flat in a gabled, three-storey Victorian property in Oxford Road, Moseley, which I understood we would be renting until his work dictated otherwise.

Our new abode was warm and welcoming. Glossy black, double front doors with a hefty iron knocker invited us into a baronial hall. With its high ceilings and original black and white tiled flooring, two bedrooms led off; one to the left for me – my father had splashed out on a new light beech dressing table and matching chest of drawers – and one to the right for my parents, again with single beds. The tall sash windows fascinated me, and I wasted no time experimenting. The sizeable lounge-cum-dining room overlooked a compact courtyard scattered with chipped terracotta pots with withered foliage. The room was bare; it had little to fill it except a small settee and two armchairs covered in hideous gold stretch covers with pulled threads from dog's claws, thoughtful hand-downs from Nancy, my father's sister. What possessions we had brought over from Cape Town had arrived out of storage but in an absence of curtains and to afford us privacy in the front of the property, my father borrowed a stepladder and tacked white sheeting to the extensive bay windows.

My mother detested the appearance. 'Looks like the slums,' she told him, 'as though we haven't got two pennies to rub together.'

'Temporary thing this. No need splashing out as we might not be here long.' I too felt embarrassed. For someone who liked to create an impression, he had let himself down.

My father's priority was to rent a television set from Radio Rentals so we could watch *Dr Who, Coronation Street* and the *Black and White Minstrel Show*. Because the introduction of television in Cape Town was after I left, this was one luxury I had never experienced, and I marvelled that we could have all the entertainment at a flick of a switch.

Our move to Moseley came with one momentous difference; Connie had not made an appearance. I thought I was dreaming when I made my discovery. I could not stop talking about it and my mother wore a permanent grin. Apart from our short spell in the hotel after leaving Newlands, I had no recollection of what it was like to be a family of three. When I plucked up the courage and asked where she had gone, my mother merely shrugged and remained tight lipped. I longed for this day and saw fun on the horizon.

Prior to our arrival, one of my father's tasks had been to locate a new school for me and Edgbaston High came up trumps, an independent day school for girls which, he said, offered the same high standard of education as Herschel.

'Say you'd like to be a teacher,' he drummed into me, in the hope it might secure me a place. I had always dreamt about this as a future career but never imagined having to use it as a bargaining tool. After a morning of exam papers, delight spread across his face when he heard I'd been successful but because we didn't start school in Cape Town until the age of six, Mr Dutton who lived a short bus journey away in Five Ways, had been recommended to provide me with some extra maths tuition on a Saturday morning.

Within a short space of time, it became apparent that school life in England was different to anything I had experienced previously. During morning break at Herschel, we filed crocodile fashion through the dining room to collect a jam sandwich laid out on an enormous tray, often quince which I detested, but with my dislike of butter mine sat on a separate plate at the side. For morning break at Edgbaston, we had the opportunity to buy a chocolate digestive biscuit for one old penny. One day, I decided to chance my luck and, dropping three pennies into the pot, I helped myself to four! That evening I was the victim of violent sickness, never sure whether it was the school Christmas dinner we had that day or because I had been dishonest.

Although I longed for my home to be a cheerful one, the morning I woke to hear a fiery discussion between my parents alarmed me and, with my hormones kicking in, there were times when my father and I did not communicate. There was little to be cheerful about, and I hoped he could see the effect it was having on me. Our strained existence prompted me to keep a chart on the back of my bedroom door to monitor the days without dialogue and with the occasional lack of conversation between my parents I'd ask my father a question so he would have to address my mother with the answer.

His pressurised job had also given him a stomach ulcer which did not help matters and the white chalky medicine prescribed by the doctor he said 'gave him the shits'. Whenever arguments spiralled, I was there to quell the storm, but he often worked late into the evening which left me and my mother on our own. She knew few people and her mundane life was taking its toll. She seldom confided in me but when she did, she would say, 'I've had enough.' Trying to console her sometimes downcast spirits, keep on the right side of my father and adapt to new challenges had become a testing time but I took comfort in the routine of school life. I concluded that growing up was difficult; or it was for me.

My relationship with my father had changed. The emotional detachment between us had grown wider. I longed to feel a connection, but his temper was short, his time limited and our personalities had begun to grate. Why was he so moody? I felt rejection and struggled with self-belief. On dreary days, I comforted myself with a Cadbury's cake – samples, of course. I consumed far too many of those cakes which meant there were far too many dreary days.

As we headed into the depths of my first frigid winter, I was ill prepared: I detested wearing my 'smart' regulation school camel coat, especially at weekends, but the alternative was a drab grey hand-down from my paternal grandmother which I disliked even more.

The rawness of that icy weather gave me a bad feeling about life in England. I recall a discussion with my mother. One evening as we sat warming ourselves in front of a roaring fire, I told her of my sad day. Because everything I once lived and breathed had been taken from me, I felt trapped in a dull suburb with little to keep me occupied. I couldn't stop thinking about my birthplace and all the friends I'd left behind; the hours spent sprawled out on sun drenched beaches when we feasted on yummy koeksisters, (twisted mouth-watering donuts infused with sweet syrup), relaxing on pool terraces, playing hide and seek amongst sun-ripened vineyards, and at the end of the day the spicy mouth-watering aromas of boerewors sizzling on the braai.

To ease matters, my mother suggested it would be a clever idea if I kept a diary so I could put my feelings down on paper. She did not have to tell me twice; I rushed to my bedroom, tore a handful of sheets from an exercise book, stapled them together and started writing.

Although I have had eight moves since my time in Moseley, my thoughts for that year have survived together with details of my first day at Edgbaston High School.

'September 1963:
Felt sick. Caught early bus. Mum came with me as it was my first morning. Felt awful telling her I didn't need her, but she insisted on escorting me to the main gate. Surrounded by hundreds of pupils in green uniform, everyone chatting about their summer holidays. Joined up with girls who deposited me at reception, like a parcel delivery. Eyes stared as though they'd never seen a new girl before. Ushered into classroom I got my nervous introductions out of the way. Teacher had a disgusting green tweed suit and looked incredibly old. Discovered I shouldn't be with the top achievers and marched off to new classroom. More gawping girls wanted to know where I'd come from. Introductions all over again. Rest of my first day not so bad. Met Margaret who lives up the road. Her dad's a vet. She's

very friendly.
Called in at local shop on way home to buy tickey frozen sucker [an Ice lolly in Cape Town's currency]. Woman behind the counter gave me a weird look.'

I had made notes on various events and in November of that year I wrote:

'Dad not speaking. What have I done??? I try not to annoy him. Just wondering am I rude? Difficult? Bad tempered? I wish I knew. All I want is a bit of fun. And Mum not happy either. I never see Dad give her a kiss. Please love us both. It's getting colder now. Trees are bare. Branches laden with frost. Just how cold does it get over here?'

And then I'd written:

'22nd November 1963:
President Kennedy shot dead today. How awful. Poor man.'

'December 1963:
I'm about to have my first Christmas. Everything reversed. It's funny seeing snow scenes on Christmas cards. Only know boiling temperatures with Christmas flowers in full bloom. (Hydrangeas I found out they're called.) Would normally be wearing shorts and running around bare foot struggling to keep cool, but now wearing layers of clothes and huddled in front of roaring fire struggling to keep warm.
Went carol singing with school friends this evening. Fingers froze. Came back to our house. Mum had made hot mince pies which we ate sat round the Christmas tree. Dad had put it in a metal bucket which I covered with a red crepe paper bow and decorated with glass baubles from Cape Town. Never done this before. Great fun.'

'January 1964:
Hate the winter. Cold all the time. Filled up coal scuttle

from brick store to help Mum. Deep drift of crunchy snow. Made snowman. Fingers and toes dead. Not a good day. Mum mentioned divorce to Dad. Made me sad. It won't be the same ever again. Now worried as don't know where I will end up and who I will live with. I'm never leaving my lovely mummy.'

Desperate to taste normality, I wanted my friend Margaret's life, where the atmosphere in her home appeared relaxed and her family enjoyed a comfortable lifestyle to which I had been accustomed. I could not understand why my father had become a mean man. From time to time I had heard mention that he would like to purchase his own business. Why work for others when you can be your own boss is what he would say, so was that the reason he seemed keen to reign in his expenditure? That gave me another dilemma. What type of business and in what direction would we be heading? Nothing appeared settled.

During my time in Birmingham, I remember abandonment being my biggest fear. All these years later, when I hear of families divorcing, I feel a familiar surge of dread for children not knowing which parent they will end up with.

'May 1964:
Just had brilliant news. Jenny coming to stay. Tidied my room and drawers. Not much in them but tried to make my clothes appear more, like Jenny's. Dad collecting her. SOOO excited.'

I recall Jenny's first words when she arrived in Moseley. 'Mum wondered if Connie would be with you.' Knowing how her thoughtful mother had so often removed me from the pressures at home, I am sure she was intrigued to know her whereabouts. It seemed that Connie was a constant source of mystery and although she was not around, I could never understand why there was still uneasiness between my parents.

After two abortive attempts to relocate back to England, along with her mother and brother, Jenny had settled in Canterbury. I think my father sensed how close our friendship had become in Cape Town when on another occasion he drove me to

Kent to spend time with her. Once again, we indulged in nostalgia, discussing the horrors of doing gym in our voluminous blue knickers and the delights of Herschel special: jam sponge cake set in custard. We visited the colossal cathedral, one of the oldest and most famous Christian structures in England, and with my pocket money I purchased a box of cream plastic cocktail sticks for my mother and a postcard which I wrote whilst sat in a pew overlooking the altar.

There was another entry that caused me a wobble:

'Grandma coming to stay. Dad cross. Icy unease.'

And then:

'GRANDMA HAS ARRIVED. Although she's eighty-two and ancient, I like having her staying. She's sharing my bedroom. Often sniffing smelling salts. Her underwear is old fashioned. Never seen anything like it. She wears a flesh coloured Spirella corset – it's torturous and body gripping with hundreds of hooks and eyes and a right palaver to get off at bedtime as she can't see that well.'
Loads of trouble. Dad at work all day, thank goodness. Sometimes comes home late. Tried to cheer Mum. Heard grandma speak to Dad in lounge this afternoon but he chose to ignore her. They've never got on.'

'Saturday:
Dad, Mum, and I visited Bull Ring in Birmingham today. Dad gave us a Cadbury's cream egg as we walked round Rackham's departmental store. Mum couldn't possibly eat hers, far too sweet!!! Loved this afternoon.'

To this day I get an ache in my stomach with this next entry:

'Mum said she couldn't go to Parents Evening although Margaret's parents pleaded. They offered her a lift, but she declined unable to tell them that the real reason was because she had nothing suitable to wear.'

My notes made fascinating reading and I adored those rare snatched times when I was alone with my parents. The most memorable of these was my trip to Edgbaston Botanical Gardens. As summer turned to autumn, and piles of golden leaves rustled beneath our feet, we skipped along like children. The delight on their faces made my heart race and to witness my father gripping my mother's hands and blowing on them to keep them warm gave me a feeling of cosiness. In my diary I wrote:

> 'It was brilliant. Just the THREE of us. Loved every second. I pray we can do this more often. Never seen them hold hands before. Amazing. Everyone happy. I'll remember it forever.'

I never imagined my notes as a fourteen-year-old could rekindle so many vivid memories decades later but twelve months after our move to Birmingham I overheard perturbing news.

'I'm afraid it'll involve another one,' my father said. He explained that Cadbury's had offered him a position he could not refuse.

'What?' My mother slammed down her coffee cup and leapt to her feet.

'Depot's in London.'

'London?' I chipped in.

'Battersea, actually. Means we'll have to find somewhere to live down that way. And it'll have to be within a twenty-mile radius as prices are ridiculous. Out of the question anything nearer.'

My stomach turned to lead as the implications began to sink in. 'What about the friends I've just made?'

'Plenty of fish in the sea,' was his response.

'Hmm … Poor Diane will have to change school *yet* again. Not good for her all this relocating, especially with O levels around the corner. Only just settled into this one.' My mother tended to express an opinion when it concerned me.

She knew that when my father had decided on something it was a fait accompli but the more she considered the prospect, the more she realized she would be nearer her ageing mother. Grandma shared her time between her other two daughters, Linda in Formby and Freda who now lived near Guildford and I think she knew it would be more convenient for her to visit.

She gave a huffy sigh. 'I hope this is the last.'

'Never know in my job.'

Finding the right house, convenient location, suitable price, and oodles of DIY opportunities did not take long.

'It's an old property. Potential written all over it,' my father assured us.

As our time in Moseley neared an end, our sturdy, well-travelled crates saw daylight once again. I was a brilliant packer; I'd had enough experience. Even my father, whose motto was nobody-does-it-as-well-as-me, put his trust in my skill.

During our time at the flat, there was never any mention of Connie's whereabouts. That was until I heard an animated discussion between my parents. With my ear pressed against the lounge door my father mentioned something along the lines that now Connie had moved to London, which started me thinking. If she hadn't been living in London, as I thought, where was she, because she did come to tea one weekend, and there was another appearance to see Bunty after his six months in quarantine had ended. Were we moving to Surrey because Connie was now there? If so, why? And, if she had been living in Birmingham while we were there, where was she working? That was my biggest quandary.

I tried to block all negative thoughts from my mind, including the mention of divorce which had given me repeated nightmares.

With another imminent move my expectations were once more raised and I began daydreaming about what this new future might hold in store for us as a family.

We needed an injection of fun to lift us out of the doldrums. My diary entry read:

> 'Hope Connie doesn't come back to live with us. She wouldn't, would she???? Prefer it without her around so I can be like my friends.'

Diane Harding

CHAPTER 12
THREAT OF A KILLING

After our short stay in Moseley I was once again bidding farewell to my home.

Squashed between a laundry basket, bread bin and an assortment of coats piled high on the back seat of our blue Ford Anglia, I sped south with my parents to Burgh Heath, a picturesque village on the fringe of the Epsom Downs, an area renowned for its expansive open countryside.

As we travelled towards a new beginning, I hoped this move would be for a longer spell and to have a little light-heartedness about the home was what I craved more than anything.

My mother and I had yet to set eyes on our new dwelling; all we knew was what a good buy it had been. Swinging off the main road, a row of dreary Victorian cottages came into view. As we bumped our way down an unmade road and took a sharp left into a cul-de-sac, tucked away at the far end I saw a house with an estate agent's board saying 'sold'.

My mother beamed as we approached.

'Well … what d'you think?' my father asked, eager for our approval.

'It's beautiful,' I shrieked, craning my neck for a better view. 'It's a proper house.'

The red-brick semi-detached with a tiled mansard roof had pale amethyst wisteria drooped over the entrance porch and the overgrown imitation well in the left-hand corner gave a cottagey feel to the place. I counted four crumbling chimney pots protruding into the bright midday sky and envisaged cosy nights huddled in front of glowing embers.

Impatient to see whether the back garden would live up to my expectations, I ran and pushed open the wrought iron side gate. I was not disappointed. Borders encircled cultivated raspberry beds and as I ran my hand over a carpet of lilac lavender, the intense fragrance made my nostrils tingle. The far end was a wilderness by comparison, but my father told us his priority was to get central heating installed before winter arrived.

As Bunty and I moseyed round the garden on that first evening and the sunset gave the treetops a burnt orange glow, I was confident this was the turning point in not just my life, but also for my parents. Clinging to a dream I refused to let go of, I felt as though I was stepping into another world; it was everything I had longed for.

With the discovery that my wish had come true I effervesced with excitement. Connie had not made an appearance. No-one said anything but, intrigued by her absence, I asked my mother where she was living. 'Better ask your father,' was all she said. But the following weekend I had my query answered when he took me to her bedsit overlooking Wimbledon Common. It was small and cramped. Everything was in one room; a wardrobe, a casual chair and a settee which converted into a bed, even a tiny kitchenette in the corner. She explained that she was working in London for a top-notch record company where she'd met famous actors including Peter Hall and that her vast collection of vinyl records required shelving; that's where my father's skills came in handy.

Prior to our arrival in Surrey, schools were once again top of the agenda, with a decision that I should attend Rosebery Grammar. With further exams and another reminder to tell the Headmistress that I wished one day to become a teacher, I secured a place here too. But with so many new schools, lasting friendships were out of the question and getting to know strangers never became any easier. I would also have to learn what my new teachers expected of me and soon discovered that I was only an average pupil. I consoled myself that hopping from one school to another was the reason my education was suffering. I had even read that children who change school three or four times in their childhood can have feelings of low self-esteem. This was my fifth so where did that leave me?

With a restless energy, my father slogged away doing endless DIY tasks round the house; even my brow-beaten mother entered the spirit with the key role of stripping decades of hideous green wallpaper in the hall assigned to me. I think the red quarry tiled floor in the kitchen was the only feature that remained untouched.

Soon after our arrival, my father organised another Cadbury's social evening and with Connie out of our lives it came as a shock to learn that he had extended an invitation for her to join us. Nothing had changed; it was as though he felt it his duty to invite her. I felt appalled to think that we would be meeting these people for the first time and wondered what they might make of it. My vexed mother did her usual tutting but in the end we all went along playing happy families. Looking back, it was obvious Connie felt relaxed at these gatherings and I speculated on whether she accompanied us for my father's sake, afraid that if she turned down his invitation, she might hurt his feelings. Even when she was not around, I could feel her presence, like a ghost hovering, waiting to cause trouble.

After six months in Surrey, things did not seem to be shaping up as I had hoped. Cracks were beginning to appear. The idyllic family life I longed for was a testing one. There were ugly periods of tension and when the going got tough, I'd suggest we go for a ramble on the downs.

On first appearances, my father appeared a gentleman, anxious to create an impression. A man who liked the best of everything, he always looked stylish with one of his fine grey woollen suits purchased from Saville Row. Personable and popular, he oozed charm to anyone who met him but beneath that façade lurked a dominant and manipulative character with a fuse that took little to ignite. 'Must be the pressure of that new job of his,' my mother declared, but whatever the reason, she found his ways impossible to cope with. I never recall him asking her opinion or advice; he was the decision maker in all things.

Brimful with common sense, there was a practicality in everything my mother tackled. She always tied a knot in her hanky as a reminder for something, but for all her organised and methodical habits lurked a delicate and fragile character. Unless my father was in one of his jocular moods, little laughter filled our cottage at Burgh Heath. To experience my parents united in their love for me and not as individuals was what I craved more than anything.

During our time in Surrey, something extraordinary happened. I wondered if I'd heard correctly when my father told us that he'd booked a holiday. The advertisement showed a caravan site overlooking expansive white sands at Sennen Cove in Cornwall. Our venture sounded idyllic. With a reservation made for the first week of the summer holidays, the following morning I bounced along to school with renewed energy. This would be my first spell away since arriving back in England and the thought of travelling through unknown countryside held my imagination.

What delighted me was my mother singing and swaying to the music on the radio but by evening I was on my bed in a heap of disappointment: I learnt that Connie would again be joining us. I was furious with people, with life and whatever came my way. It seemed there was nothing we could do as a family without this person continually tagging along.

Nothing of significance about my time at Sennen stands out, except that there were four of us in a cramped, damp and rusty caravan, I bought a pair of navy-blue mirrored sunglasses, (I have a photograph wearing them, clad in a navy swimming costume, sitting on a boulder, looking miserable) and we travelled to nearby Mousehole for our evening meals. What made the most impression on me was driving past Stonehenge on our homeward journey – back in those days, the main through route was via the ancient monument – and to stop, take in its splendour and learn about its early history had me fascinated.

My sanity during this time was huddling under the bedclothes at night with headphones suctioned to my ears listening to Radio Luxemburg. I'd become a fan of the Beatles and the Hollies, and, with an occasional purchase of the *New Musical Express* magazine to keep me up to date with their latest hits, my father was quick to show his exasperation. 'What d'you want to buy that rubbish for?' he would chide whenever he spied a copy lying around. 'Waste of money.' I wanted to tell him it was for a bit of light relief but knew I would regret it. But for my sixteenth birthday, he softened, and I became the proud owner of a Dansette record player, as the gramophone we had in Cape Town had not made it over to England. I caressed the smooth leatherette exterior and wondered what I had done to deserve it. With enough pocket money saved, my first vinyl purchase was The Seekers' *A World of Our Own,* played incessantly until the hole in the middle became enlarged. On the rare occasions when I invited my school friends to tea there was little else with which to gain a bit of 'cred'.

Although my mother's life had become an emotional roller coaster, she did everything in her powers to appease my father by preparing soused herrings and brawn, two of his favourites, and on a Saturday morning, she'd catch the bus to MacFisheries in Sutton to buy rabbit for a stew which he adored.

Once again, the good times I longed for had not materialised.

And, things were about to get worse.

One evening as I sat at the dining table tackling my maths homework I heard my mother talking on the phone.

'Who's that?' It sounded as though someone was coming to stay.

'Grandma,' she said. 'Need to give Freda a break for a couple of weeks. It's ten months since she stayed with us in Birmingham. Besides, it'll be good to have company while you're at school.'

'Oh my God. Couple of weeks?' I shuddered at the thought. I had visions of the storm it caused the last time she visited. 'Don't like the sound of it,' I told her. 'And neither will Dad. He doesn't like her. In fact, I think he hates her.'

'D'you know what? I don't care. It's lonely here during the day.'

Her pending visit I knew would cause an explosion. My stubborn father still harboured a grudge since those early days in Cape Town. For my mother, it was a tough call. She felt it only fair she took her turn but at the same time risked a worsening situation at home. I loved my grandma and I knew my mother would benefit from the company. I had not grown up with grandparents, so part of me was looking forward to the arrival of this placid, quietly spoken lady.

'So, what did Dad say when you told him?' I was eager to know his reaction.

It seemed my mother had played him at his own game by

not forewarning him of Grandma's pending visit until she'd arrived. I figured that must be the reason for the commotion in the front room. It was one of those instances where it was better to steer clear and say nothing. I switched off the radio and managed to catch the tail end of the heated discussion.

'Only a couple of weeks … give Freda a break.'

'Is she!'

It sounded vicious and I had no intention of hanging around. I'd been sitting in the dining room with my feet up in the armchair but before I could escape my mother entered and squeezed in beside me.

My father followed and stood in the doorway. 'Took it for granted, did you?' he said, his eyebrows scrunched, and his shirt sleeves pushed up to his elbows. 'With not as much as a "do you mind"?' Compared to the earlier brightness of the afternoon his thunderous tones had plunged the day into darkness.

'Well, even-stevens. Like you consulted me before Connie came to stay all those years ago.' She was taking a chance.

I leapt out of the chair. 'Don't be so horrid to poor Mum.' I could not take any more of his bullying. She did not deserve it. I was a sensitive child, always had been, so he'd know his behaviour would upset me. I studied this man in dismay, wondering how we had gone from those early perfect times to this.

The bickering continued.

Like a monster about to pounce my father took several strides towards my mother. 'I'll kill you!' He raised his clenched fist. I had never heard anything as violent as that threat and judging by the tone of his voice he was a whisker away from it. My mother's face was the colour of putty. Wide eyed she backed away.

'Calm down Vic, *will* you,' she pleaded, trying to inject a little normality into a senseless situation. 'Become quite out of hand. Just because Mother's staying doesn't mean we need all this aggro.'

And then he stormed off to the kitchen to fill the kettle and slammed the cupboard with such force that the door fell off its hinges. 'Serves him right,' my mother mumbled. I prayed the neighbours had not heard his outburst.

I fled upstairs and to drown out my fear turned on my transistor radio. Surely, he wouldn't. Would he? It was like a drama, our back room the stage. Growing up in that toxic environment was difficult; my father was like living with a human volcano waiting to erupt. By early evening he was still ranting. 'Right, fine,' he said as he flung open the French door and pounded into the back garden.

That was the last time we heard him speak; his non-communication spell lasted for the duration of Grandma's stay. Not appearing at mealtimes, like a recluse he took refuge in the garage, eating his meals off a makeshift, paint-flaking door. I detested having to function as go-between and waitress meals out to him; for fear he might ask me something I might find awkward, I would dump the tray and make a hasty exit.

The day before Grandma's departure was like no other. We'd finished our evening meal, my father in the garage, my mother, grandma, and me in the dining room. As we cleared away the plates the back door burst open, my father's top lip taut as he barged into the dining room. We watched open mouthed.

'I'm leaving,' he broadcast. There was silence. No-one protested. He thundered down the stairs carrying an old tartan grip and scooped his car keys from the brass ashtray on the hall table. The roar of the car engine confirmed his departure.

'Phew,' my shaken mother croaked, as though she had thrown Atlas off her shoulder. She flung her arms around me, but I wished his departure had come sooner. The days before my father's exodus had, I think, been the most tumultuous I had ever experienced.

I remember thinking, I am sixteen and my father has walked out.

As the final weak sunshine filtered into the dining room through the gap in the trees, I pondered the circumstances, thankful it was not my mother who had been the one to storm off. I wondered where my father had gone but think my mother had realized it would be to Wimbledon Common.

Grandma buried her head in her hands and said nothing, no doubt reflecting on those early days and her misgivings about her daughter marrying my father in the first place, let alone following him to Cape Town.

I heard my mother's sigh of relief from across the room and

knew that from now on, we were free to do as we pleased. No longer would we have to suffer his rage and his finicky ways with meals. I would now be at liberty to buy my *NME* magazine without a lecture and I could enjoy listening to Radio Luxemburg without someone bellowing to turn off Elvis the Pelvis. I also started to think about the black jumper I had been eyeing up in Woolworths which my father said was far too old for me.

He was gone, gone, gone. War had ended.

'Let's have a sherry,' my mother suggested with a cheerfulness in her voice I'd not heard in a long time. After our second schooner, the three of us were hysterical. This was the turning point I had dreamt about. How rapidly an unpleasant atmosphere can change. Things could only get better.

Although my father hadn't been gone long, we revelled in the peace. Happy thoughts roamed in my head and I felt positive about the future.

It was late and, not being able to sleep, I loitered at my bedroom window. I felt the cool air on my cheek through the cracked windowpane and gazed up at a sky pinpricked with stars before heaving my emotionally spent body between the sheets. Switching off Radio Luxembourg, I lay my head on the pillow and drifted off.

I woke with a jolt and peered over to my bedside table. I could see it was just past midnight by the fluorescent hands on my travel clock. A paralysing fear took hold of me. I recognised the rough sound of my father's Anglia.

Dear God. I slipped back between the sheets and hoped I was dreaming but the slam of the car door followed by the bang of the front door with equal force told me he was back. Hells bloody bells. 'I'm leaving' he had said.

As quickly as we had been handed our freedom, he had snatched it from us. I saw hope and happiness on the horizon. Where he had gone, he didn't say, but, wherever it was, it hadn't lasted.

Torrential rain greeted us the following morning.

The threatening clouds that so often swirled overhead had returned.

CHAPTER 13
A FAMILY OF FOUR, AGAIN

I was now sixteen. Life became a little quieter. Grandma had returned home, and I had heard nothing of Connie. And to see my father smiling made a refreshing change. That was until breakfast one morning.

'I don't know how to tell you darling, but your dad's been offered a different job with Cadbury's.'

'Hope you're joking!' The thought of starting afresh took my breath away.

'Wish I was. It's in Somerset,' she continued, as though I would jump at the prospect.

'I'm sick of it.' I leapt from the kitchen table. When *was* all this moving going to stop?

Trying to inject a little magic into our new venture, my father explained, 'It'll mean me having to accept the position before we've sold. If you and Diane can find a buyer for this house, I'll buy you both a watch.' Blimey. My mother and I stared at him open mouthed, flabbergasted by his generosity. It was the best offer we had ever had. My father did have a different side to him when it suited. 'I've found a property in a little village called Saltford. A pretty spot with the river Avon running through and only about four miles outside Bath. It's an elegant detached house, requiring a little work, but not nearly so much as this one,' he assured us. You'll love it.' He beamed as he explained how he had seen the property advertised for auction in a Bath estate agency.

'And I've had my offer accepted prior to it going under the hammer.'

Since my dreams for happiness had not materialised at our two previous abodes, I wondered what our new address would hold in store for us as a family. It seemed I was always chasing the impossible so all I could do was cross my fingers.

In July 1966, the day before the World Cup, we graced Saltford with our presence. The following day, we sat on rolled up carpets munching ham sandwiches, glued to the football on our little telly as my father jiggled the antenna in all directions to bring the match into sharper focus.

Although he had kept his promise and presented both my mother and me with our gold watches, after our reward came punishment. My father was back to his old tricks.

The following morning my mother stomped into my bedroom.

'She's back!' She swished open the curtains. I shot up in bed, half dazed.

'What?' My stomach churned. 'Connie's back?'

'Bloody cheek. Like it's her God-given right. And no mention of it,' she said, storming out of the room.

I began to wonder if this person was the reason for our constant uprooting; was it my father who encouraged Connie to return or was it Connie who ingratiated herself into my family? Or were we following her? Who was chasing who? I came up with another theory. Perhaps my father felt sorry for her never having had a father figure in her life. Whichever way, she showed no embarrassment; living her life with an unbelievable lack of awareness that must have incensed my mother.

Within weeks of her arrival, she had secured a part-time position in the local chemist. What troubled me was whether she told people she lived with us and what they might think. Were these people judging my home? I had already overheard the next-door neighbour enquiring about her. Connie had been with us for fourteen years, aside from a short spell while we were living in Birmingham and Surrey.

My father's outbursts had not evaporated and when things got the better of my mother, she would resort to the same words.

'Surely, Diane, you can see this is not a normal existence?' And then she would ask, 'Do you know how unhappy it's making me?' My heart melted whenever I heard those words and I tried never to engage for fear she would tell me she was leaving; I'd lived with the constant threat of her one day packing her bags since I'd heard the mention of divorce when we lived in Birmingham.

One evening, while living in Saltford, I told Connie that I didn't think it advisable to get married. I was adamant I was not going to fall into the trap as it did not make for a happy future.

'Causes too many problems. Look at poor Mum. She's never cheerful.' With my mother out of earshot, it seemed a perfect opportunity to say what I thought. I wanted Connie to believe me and I didn't hold back letting her know how she was suffering. My sudden outburst shocked me, but I had wanted to offload my feelings for a considerable time.

'Goodness Di Di. Don't adopt that attitude.' I felt her eyes drilling into mine.

'People need people,' she went on. 'That's what girls dream about don't they? Getting married one day?'

'Well, *you* haven't!' In my head I told myself it would be far simpler. I'd be answerable to nobody and could come and go as I pleased and not allow myself to be imprisoned like my mother had been for as long as I could remember. What's more, I didn't need Connie to lecture me on what to do with my life.

'It doesn't always work out that way,' she said. 'Life can be complicated and besides, Mr Right might not always be available.'

Hearing her talk like that disturbed me. If only I could have read her thoughts and asked her what she meant. I went to bed that night with her remarks on my mind. Who was this Mr Right?

Living in Somerset meant there were unfamiliar places to explore and one of these was Rode Bird Gardens. My mother and Connie shared a passion for birds, so this outing was a definite. I dreaded any excursion but for once the mood was cheerful and relaxed with everyone chatting as we sauntered through the colourful gardens. Even my father, who seldom struck up conversation with strangers, appeared eager to explain to a group of Chinese visitors that we lived with the scenic River Avon on our doorstep.

When the sweltering mid-day temperature called for re-
freshments, with a purposeful stride my father went off to make
his purchases. He'd chosen a Lyons ice cream but when he discovered he would have to buy a whole pack of wafers to sandwich
it together, disgusted, he hurled the lot in the bin, unable to understand why he should pay for six when two would do. So that
was that, wafers in the bin and an atmosphere. If he could not get
his own way, he made it known.

I was now seventeen and beginning to taste freedom. To put
my troubles behind me and live in the present gave me a new
lease of life. Not only had I been successful in acquiring the position as a Saturday sales assistant in a lighting shop in Bath – I was
paid two pounds for a day's work which was considerably more
than other places offered – but I had also met Heather, who lived
at the top of our road. With smiley features and enormous enquiring eyes, we shared the same birthday and although she was two
years younger than me, we discovered that we had enrolled on
the same secretarial course in the same college. With a smattering
of 'O' level qualifications I'd gained at the grammar school not
sufficient to set me on the road to any great profession (there was
only one person to blame for that), it was enough for me to register on my course.

The Swinging Sixties produced mods and rockers on Vesper
scooters and roaring motorbikes, Mary Quant shift dresses and
flared trousers. I remember saving my hard-earned money to
purchase a pair of bright red bell-bottom jeans and my father telling me they looked ridiculous. It was also a time to experiment in
drugs and free sexual exploits but putting temptation aside,
Heather and I preferred to admire the two-wheeled machines in
preference to their owners.

Having struck up a close friendship with Heather, on Friday
evenings we would sometimes take ourselves off to the Bath Pavil-
ion to see well known groups such as The Who, The Rolling
Stones and The Kinks or occasionally a crowd of us from college
would venture into Bristol for discos at the Locarno or Corn Ex-
change. To leave the drudgery of home life behind was
exhilarating. I had never had it so good and revelled in my independence.

With Connie part of our household, intrigue continued to

follow us around. Every move had produced the same curiosity and our new surroundings brought renewed explanations. Although it was there for everyone to see, I felt uncomfortable. I dreaded people asking and would pretend I hadn't heard. It was none of their business, so I avoided the question at all costs. Looking back, it was obvious my father was oblivious what others thought.

It wasn't long after our move to the West Country that Heather questioned me about Connie. Her parents were intrigued with her presence and, because she had one slightly drooping eyelid, wanted to know whether she'd been a spy with the Secret Service and had saved my father's life and that this was his indebted gratitude to her. I presumed they were joking and found it amusing to think that people brandished scenarios about like that, all of them at the expense of my home. I never recall Connie meeting Heather's parents although it was obvious their paths had crossed at some point.

When I recently met up with her, four decades later, we picked up from where we'd left off, pooling memories and reminiscing about the Sixties. We discussed Connie at great length and laughed till we cried at the tale her parents had conjured up. I was also interested to hear Heather's take on my mother. She said she found her 'a quiet and private lady, classy and composed, just ladylike and lovely'. My chest filled with pride to think it was my mother she was talking about.

I envied Heather. When she successfully passed her driving test, it gave us the freedom to venture down to the nearby Blagdon Lakes in her father's red Mini Cooper. Driving lessons with my father had not been as successful; although he took me out practising in his silver Cortina GT, patience was not his thing; however, the thrill of being behind the wheel more than compensated for his shortcomings. One of the most memorable trips during my novice days, and I guess it was his too, was when I attempted a nearby roundabout. Unsure how to make my exit I had circled it more times than my father thought necessary.

'We stuck in a groove or something? Now, when you're ready.' So, the next time round I thought I would go for it. And with a sharp lurch left I cut in front of the vehicles following behind and proceeded down the bypass.

'Christ! he exclaimed; his knuckles white as he pulled his knees up under his chin. 'Wrong bloody lane!' he screeched, as horns beeped and two fingers pointed in the air. Producing a hanky to mop his brow, we had made it. We were home and dry by a whisker. But somehow, and I cannot for the life of me think how, I managed to repeat the same manoeuvre the following day!

My mother had been applying for job vacancies in Bath and accepted a position as cashier in Burton's, the men's outfitters. My father didn't share her enthusiasm, but she told me, 'I couldn't care less. It's my decision and nothing to do with him. It'll give me freedom and finally a little income to call my own.' It was an opportunity she had longed for and it would be the making of her, she said.

Living in Saltford proved not all gloom and doom. In the summer of 1969, I too was beginning a new phase in my life. I had met Christopher Harding, a talented twenty-year-old sportsman whose weekends were football in winter and cricket in summer and, back in those days, when you were in the Somerset second eleven sandwiched in the batting order between Ian Botham and Viv Richards, there was every good reason to put girls on the back burner. Doris, his mother, urged him to see what was out there apart from sport; that's when he quick-stepped into my life at ballroom dancing lessons at the Forum in Bath, a let-your-hair-down Saturday gathering that Heather and I often frequented.

For the first time since arriving in England I realized there was something out there called fun; a whole new life was beginning to unfurl.

Although Chris was from a conventional family, like me, he was an only child. He was good company and had a playful personality but most important he was someone my father found acceptable. I remember that sunny Sunday afternoon when my mother and I strolled along the winding banks down by the River Avon and I dropped his name into the conversation.

'Sounds a delightful chap,' she said, beaming. 'I'm so pleased for you.' It thrilled me to see her happy.

Although holidays were not my father's priority, he returned from work one evening and caught us by surprise. With his briefcase still clutched under his arm he announced that he planned to give us a treat by taking us away to Laredo in northern Spain, an experience that would involve catching an overnight ferry.

'Do us good to have a break.' I think he thought he was giving us a treat of a lifetime.

For once I agreed with him and wondered whether he was missing the South African sunshine. Because there had been little to enthuse about on our trip to Cornwall, I hoped this next excursion would prove more memorable for the right reasons.

I thought my heart would explode at the thought of being away with my parents for two long weeks. Although I had lived abroad for fourteen years, going on holiday was a novelty. I told everyone at college and was impatient for August to arrive, but I could tell my mother did not share in my enthusiasm.

'Not keen,' she whispered in my ear over breakfast the following morning. 'Besides, I don't seem to be such a good sailor these days.'

Shortly after learning that we were to venture abroad, at the dinner table one evening Connie mentioned that she needed to renew her passport.

'Passport? Intrigued I asked what far flung corner of the world she would be visiting.

'Spain!' She ruffled her eyebrows as though it was obvious.

I felt sick and stomped off into the back garden to contain my rage.

I went to bed that night calling my father every expletive I knew but by the morning I had come up with a cunning plan. I mustered the courage and asked him,

'What would you say if Chris came with us?'

He bit his bottom lip, as though trying to figure out the feasibility of my request.

I crossed my fingers and awaited the verdict.

'That's an excellent idea.' He patted my shoulder. 'It'll be company for you.' I could not stop talking about it and that went for Chris, too, as it would be his first trip abroad.

Our two-bedroomed apartment opened onto inviting ivory sands with a breath-taking vista of iridescent ocean. Again, it involved me sharing with Connie, with Chris sleeping on the converted settee in the lounge.

I never did ascertain whether my father anticipated a food shortage in the shops, but he thought it would be sensible to take a plentiful supply of tinned meatballs. 'Just in case,' he said. Not only that but also Cracker Barrel cheddar. As it happened, there were no food shortages, with our first purchase an enormous bottle of Martini, poured into a teapot to aid dispensing. We had three meals of meatballs; my father made sure we were not taking them back. Chris told me afterwards how he detested the things.

I found myself reminiscing with him recently about that first holiday we spent together. He reminded me how, on the outward journey, we had all gone to the bar in the evening with my mother unable to join us because she felt seasick. Although Connie was laughing and enjoying her beer, he said he felt sorry my mother was not with us to share in the fun. Aware that Chris did not know everything about my home life, I speculated what he had made of this person always accompanying us.

This wasn't the only topic we ended up discussing. I reminded him of the invitation to his twenty-first birthday celebration at his parents' home. I remember the smell of freshly baked sausage rolls that wafted towards us as we stepped into the hall and the loud chatter and laughter that emanated from the front room to the accompaniment of swing music from the gramophone in their bay window. As we entered that front room, a hush descended. Heads turned and I felt the colour rush to my cheeks when I saw Chris's mother give an impressive roll of her eyes. It was another instance when my father took it for granted that Connie would join us. One thing led to another and then Chris recapped when Connie's sister, Viv, and her husband, Bill, had visited us in Saltford and how we had all gone out to Sunday dinner. I hadn't known him long, so not only was he trying to figure out Connie's association with my family, but he wondered what Viv had thought about her living with us.

Chris was from a conventional family. The first time I met his mother was after she had returned from choir practice with the Mother's Union. I was impressed and felt intimidated, knowing I didn't have a good singing voice myself. Bustling and energetic, and judging by the photographs with a figure a little fuller than in her youth, Doris had an enviable peach-like complexion. And I shall never forget my initial introduction to Bill, his father. Still wearing his carpenter's apron tied round his lean frame and a pencil tucked behind his ear, he exclaimed that I looked like Lulu, the well-known singer from Scotland who rose to fame in the Sixties. I took that as a compliment and from then on, that was how he referred to me.

When I think back to my home life, it was obvious it was a weird one. Of course, at the time, I had no idea what was to come. In my maturity, it was unbelievable to think my father had caused my mother so much misery, as though unaware of her existence at times.

I was now twenty and just when my life was beginning to take an upward turn, the mellow summer of that year brought with it renewed agony. These troubles were on an emotional level that I had not experienced before.

And, I had only myself to blame.

Diane Harding

CHAPTER 14
THE LIFT

S ince arriving in England, my life had taken countless tricky
turns, and this was another of those bumpy routes I would
need to navigate.

With both of us working on Saturdays, my mother and I
would catch the bus into Bath to our respective jobs. With a chill
winter rain lashing against our raincoats, we broke out into a
sprint but arrived too late. As we watched the bus pull away, a
maroon Ford Anglia swung into the lay-by.

'Like a lift?' A male driver with a softly spoken voice called
through the passenger window.

My mother appeared grateful that someone had offered to
pick us up. 'Nice to know there are some thoughtful folk out
there,' she whispered later that evening when we were making our
bedtime drink. And I thought no more about it.

My mother's employment in Bath had offered her a new
lease of life and it seemed she was after more. The idea of night
school appealed, so she enrolled on a dressmaking course at the
local secondary school.

'It's years since I've sat behind a sewing machine.' Her eyes
sparkled with enthusiasm.

'Don't blame you,' I told her. I thought it sounded a splendid
idea as it would get her out of the house at least one evening a
week. It pleased me that she was thinking of herself for once.

It was here, soon after starting, that I discovered she had met up with the gentleman who had gallantly stopped to offer us a lift on that soggy Saturday. Harold Dowsett, Howard to my mother as she detested the name Harold, was on an 'Improve your French' course, whether by design or coincidence I had no idea.

Thereafter, Howard picked us up from the bus stop and drove my mother and me into Bath every Saturday morning. Soon after they had met, there was a journey I recall; with a glint in their eyes and their shoulders leaning towards each other, they appeared comfortable in one another's company with an electrical spark between them that made me suspicious. There was something going on and it made me feel uneasy. Preoccupied with his female passenger, Mr D (that was how I referred to him) had become oblivious that he was still in second gear. I sat in the back fearful the car might blow up as we travelled the four-mile journey into Bath.

It wasn't long after that memorable journey that my mother hinted to me that she was considering leaving home. She said that she had already found herself accommodation in Bath, but I put my selfish hat on and did all in my power to persuade her to stay. When my father found out he promised her that things at home would improve and although she had heard those rash statements all too often in the past, she abandoned her plans.

As though intoxicated by freedom, my mother's chance meeting set in motion a chain of reactions over which I would have no control. It was obvious I now had competition. I viewed their liaison as a threat which might dislocate my family home and my security. Tricky as things were, we were still a unit, if only hanging by a delicate thread. I envisaged the collapse of the strong bond I shared with my mother and the prospect unnerved me. This feeling of jealousy was new, and I wished it would go away. My mother was the only person I could confide in. Unable to talk to anyone, least of all my father, this was a dilemma I would have to face on my own.

Meanwhile, although still employed by Cadbury's, my father's long-term ambition to purchase a business had again reared its head and by the summer of 1969 he had stumbled on a lucrative Post Office, News and Confectionery shop in Sea Mills, one he said that had everything to offer and, convinced it was the right decision, he handed in his notice at Cadbury's.

As the long summer days turned into darkened nights, with a melancholy heart, we relocated to a mediocre semi amongst screaming kids in an area to which we would have to adapt. To improve the exterior appearance, within days my father had painted the front door a cheerful canary yellow and, on either side, had planted standard rose trees in holes dug big enough to accommodate a horse.

'Peace, this variety's called,' he informed me. Peace? I thought he was having a laugh.

'Isn't there one called trouble?' I enquired. I knew as soon as I asked the question it was a mistake.

'Look,' he said, shaking his forefinger under my nose. 'No need to be insolent.'

Although with every move I found myself bargaining with God for a brighter future, by now I knew the answer.

Moving further away from Chris was not the only thing on my mind; the thought of my mother's new acquaintance posed a constant threat. I hoped it would not mean she was going to forsake me, although I asked myself whether the distance between them would mean the end of their friendship. I had no idea what to think and tried to block such thoughts from my mind.

My father's enthusiasm for his new adventure proved far greater than anything my mother and I could muster. But the crisis came when he announced that he had appointed Connie as postmistress in the business.

'You what?' My mother thumped her fist on the kitchen table with such force that the bruise lasted for days. 'Why *her* when you know how capable I am with figures? That's what I do at work, isn't it?' My mother was brilliant with figures, something my father would have been aware of; even back in the days when they'd first met, she worked in an accountancy office.

Her face turned ashen and I thought she would explode. To hear her voice her opinion with such venom was unusual but for her it was the final humiliation. I now knew that, with this appointment, Connie would not be leaving any time soon. And my mother knew it too and, although a mistake, she confronted my father.

'It's time for Connie to walk.' He had always been impossible to talk to, but she summoned up the courage to ask if he would agree to a divorce. To hear that dreaded word was like a punch in the gut and it was at times like these that I prayed I was invisible.

His face reddened. 'You must be crazy,' he sniggered. I could cry when I think back to those agonising circumstances.

After that show-down there was little communication between my parents. I knew my mother had been to the doctor complaining of headaches, but Connie took the mounting tension in her stride, wrapped up in her own thoughts and feelings. Looking back, I wondered whether she and my father had schemed a plot in the hope my mother would eventually leave. If that was the case, it seemed ironic to think that, over the years, she had prayed for Connie to pack her bags.

Life without my mother would be unimaginable; we needed one another. But she had given my father an ultimatum and, from what I had overheard, it seemed he could not allow himself to tell Connie she would have to find alternative accommodation. That's tough, I thought. I could never understand why she didn't live in the empty flat above the shop. And to hear my father tell my mother he loved her was absurd.

'You've got a strange way of showing it!' she retaliated. Trapped in an abusive relationship she had become shackled to the house. To manage her frustration, she would sometimes hum to a tune on the radio.

Two things happened soon after our move to Sea Mills. My father fell out with his next-door neighbour, Mr Bunny, who objected to our Maltese poodle cocking his leg against his low privet hedge. From that day on the two men did not communicate.

The second occurred when I was preparing for bed one evening. I heard a strange noise outside my upstairs bedroom window. I was not imagining it. I stood motionless and listened. It came again, this time with a heavier thud against the windowsill. I peered through the tiny chink in the curtain and in the darkness saw the chilling whites of two eyes. The air sucked out of me and my heart rate quickened. I managed a scream. My father ran to investigate. 'There's a peeping tom.' He flew down the stairs two at a time, flung open the front door and rushed to the rear of the house. He seized the ladder, wobbled it and the offender, a young male in his twenties, leapt to the ground. Undaunted by his youthfulness and strapping physique my father gave chase, grabbed his arm and with a balled fist landed a severe uppercut to his jaw. Convinced he had broken it, thereafter he examined every bloke who came in his shop for bruising, not that I could imagine the culprit daft enough to venture anywhere near. I was as disgusted as I was horrified to think someone had been studying my every move. What had felt a safe place now felt frightening.

I had now accepted a full-time position at Redland Teacher Training College and my mother had secured a part time position in the accounts office at Hornes the men's retailers in Bristol, and on her days off, with reluctance, she assisted in the business serving the customers in her usual polite manner. Anything to keep the peace, she would say.

In the flower-power summer of 1970, after I'd now known Chris for twelve months, we took ourselves off to Guernsey for a week's holiday and while there announced our engagement, although not before he had requested my father's permission. Posing the question filled me with dread. I knew he thought well of him, but I had no idea how he would react to him as a future son-in-law. With butterflies in my stomach I studied the pair of them at the bottom of the garden locked in conversation under the dappled shade of the apple tree.

My mother jumped for joy at our happy news. 'I always dreamt you'd be lucky in love,' she said. I could never understand why she appeared so elated that I was about to build a life of my own with the man of my dreams but, in my maturity, I realized it was the moment she had been waiting for.

One day after returning from her stint in the shop she informed me that she could no longer continue helping.

'I've decided I need a break, so I'm off to visit Mother.' It came as no surprise. She looked drawn and I was worried for her wellbeing. 'It'll be an opportunity to get away from the pressures at home.' And her warring nerves would benefit too, she explained.

Although I praised her for her courage, the thought of not having her around filled me with horror.

'Just enjoy your break.' I insisted.

'Probably be a week,' she told me.
And I believed her.

CHAPTER 15
A NIGHTMARE DISCOVERY

Monday, 20 November 1970. My diary read:
'Worst day of my life.'

The entry went on:

> 'Caught bus to work as usual. Mum due home later but no call to say what time.'

By late afternoon, the darkened sky and biting chill matched my reluctance to return to a place I hated. I had taken the longest route home and when I spied the upright rose trees with their heads hung low in the gusty conditions my heart rate quickened.

I tiptoed the last few yards down the garden path, as though someone was watching me. My trembling hand reached for the ice-cold brass knocker. I held my breath and inched open the front door.

And then I froze in my tracks.

My eyes darted from one side of the hall to the other. The crammed bookcase looked a little less cluttered and my mother's blue silk scarf draped over the back of the rocker when I left for work that morning had vanished. I flew up the stairs two at a time and yanked open her wardrobe door. I opened my eyes and saw nothing. My heart stopped. It was the moment I had dreaded.

Each time I swiped at my tears my eyes filled again. I agonised for her. I needed to speak to her. Where was she? Was she safe?

My world had crashed. I could not understand why she would leave me in the place she knew I loathed.

I bolted to my bed for comfort and there on my pillow were two white envelopes. One addressed to 'Diane', the other, to my horror, to my father.

I mustered courage and prised open my letter:

'My dearest Diane,
I have for a long while now felt very, very unhappy. No doubt you have seen this to be so. What you may not have seen, or even guessed, is that my present miserable existence is slowly and surely destroying my self confidence, so much so, that I have come to feel desperately afraid of the future.

It would be foolish for me to pretend that the present unhappy state of affairs is of recent happening. It is unlikely that there will be any change for the better in the future.

I firmly believe your Father will continue to treat my presence with callous indifference and my fears are that this will inevitably lead to my complete mental breakdown.

You know well that I have tried to be patient, even to accepting, for your sake, the peculiar circumstances of our home life, but I am now very tired.

Dearest Diane, you have in the past, on occasions when you father's particular tirade against me had brought me to the brink of despair, sought to prevent me from leaving home and I have respected your wishes. But the years are now passing between us and I am now that much older. Soon I will be too old, whereas you will, by the grace of God, be joined with Christopher in starting a home of your own. Then I shall not have you to give me comfort or support.

I have, therefore, decided (rightly or wrongly) to make a long overdue fresh start for myself and will be living in Bath. This decision has not been an easy one to make and I have thought anxiously on the circumstances that could possibly follow, particularly in respect of the difficulties that lie ahead in making this new start.

I am hoping you will not judge me hastily, at least not until I have had an opportunity of speaking to you personally on the reasons for my actions. Please believe me I wish to cause you as little distress as possible. I have funds for my present needs, a promise of a job and several offers of furnished accommodation.

You know how much I love you darling and don't ever forget that.

Naturally, I would wish my letter to you to remain personal.

Please forgive me dear.

Your loving mother. Xx

PS I have written separately to your father.'

I burst into tears yet again. It was a pathetic letter. My poor mother: she must have been at her wits end.

Puffy red eyes glared back at me in my dressing table mirror.

I knew how difficult it must have been for her to write those words and from the tone of it how she must have agonised over her decision to pluck up the courage and leave, praying I would not think badly of her.

It hit me that our mother/daughter partnership was a deep dependency I had come to rely on. But I would have to remove my blinkers, not be selfish and look at the bigger picture. I realized I had tried to shy away from the inevitable for so long but, now she had fled, I would have to face reality and, what's more, accept it.

The fact my mother had disappeared felt like bereavement and I knew the words in her letter would haunt me forever.

And this letter for my father … I envisaged all-out war when he opened it.

When I heard the key turn in the lock, I broke out in a sweat. The front door opened then clicked shut, Connie's high-pitched greeting for the dog was familiar. It was five thirty-five. I could set my watch to her four-minute saunter back home after another day behind the post office counter with her makeup and lipstick as fresh as when she'd walked out of the house at eight forty-five that morning. It was hammering down, had been for the best part of the afternoon and I could just make out the rustle as she removed her dripping Dannimac and hung it in the cloakroom to dry.

I counted the high heel click clacks on the stripped hardwood flooring. There were nine of them before the lounge door handle slowly turned. I braced myself.

'Oh! You made me jump,' she said, her hands clasped against her chest. 'Thought you were out. Why didn't you call when I came in?' Her tan leather shoulder bag dropped at her feet with a thud. 'What's up Di Di?' She sidled up for a closer inspection of my blood-shot eyes. 'What's happened?' She put a hand on my shoulder.

I backed off. 'It's Mum. She's gone.' I could scarcely speak.

'What d'you mean, *gone*?'

'Left,' was the only word that tumbled out. I prised a sodden letter from my skirt pocket and flapped it in front of her. 'And there's one for Dad.'

'She wouldn't do that.' Her brow puckered as she considered the prospect.

'Well she has,' I snivelled, patting my eyes dry one more time. '*And* cleared her wardrobe.'

'I cannot believe Blanche would do this to you.'

'And judging by what she's written it sounds as though she's been at her wits end,' I blubbered. 'Says she'll have a breakdown if she continues to live here and I don't want to see her have to go through that nightmare again.'

I thought I'd hammer home the point just how unwell she'd been feeling and that nothing seemed to have improved between her and my father over the years and that, if anything, things are worse. I don't know why I thought it necessary, but I found myself touching on the incident when we lived in Saltford when she had tried to leave, and because of my pleading she abandoned the idea.

'Guess she's been planning this one for some time,' I told her, 'although she never said anything to me.' I shook my head in disbelief as the meaning of it began to hit home. My mother had left and would not be coming back.

I detected a glimmer of a smile as though Connie felt sorry

for me, as though she wanted me to know things would work out, but I did not need her to tell me that. She held out her arms to offer comfort, but I did not need her sympathy either. What I wanted was for her to tell me *she* was leaving and then perhaps life would return to something near normal but that would be nothing short of a miracle. It was her fault that things had got so out of hand. The fact she was still living with us and this whole thing about her being postmistress was the final straw for my mother. I had even seen her looking tearful, this sensitive soul who would camouflage her torment with silence. I knew she was struggling. And Connie must have known it. I could never understand why she didn't take her feelings into account. It must have been obvious to my father too, but he refused to acknowledge it.

'And now I've got to face the music when Dad gets in. You know how horrible he'll be when I tell him.' Connie stood there chewing her thumb nail, a habit that infuriated me.

'He's not in a particularly good mood. Caught a bloke making off with a handful of girlie magazines about an hour ago. Went after him like a deer but he got away.'

Bad mood? That was all I needed. My father had never been the easiest of people to talk to. Sometimes it would take me days to pluck up courage and approach him, especially if it were over a matter that concerned my mother.

'For goodness sake, why can't they just get on?' I was taking a chance talking to Connie like this, but I was seeing it from my mother's point of view. 'I'm fed up with the depressing atmosphere in this place. So perhaps she is better off out of it.' I hadn't intended talking about her, but I couldn't stop myself. I felt better for airing my feelings.

I looked at my watch. I wanted to put off the evil moment but knew my father would be home any minute. I paced the front room waiting for his cream Cortina to swing into the drive after depositing the day's takings into the bank's night safe on the village square.

I'd rehearsed word for word what I was going to say as soon as he walked through the door. I would get it over and scarper.

The slam of the car door and squeaking hinges on the painted side gate gave me warning. My father entered the kitchen, the doorway framing his weary silhouette. He flung his jacket on the back of the chair and carried his cup of tea into the lounge. I smiled up at him and took a deep breath, but nothing came out, as though my speaking mechanism had dried up. I licked my lips and tried again.

'Mum's left this for you. Found it on my pillow when I got in from work.' I struggled to fight back the tears as my trembling hand dangled the crumpled envelope under his nose. I watched as he slumped in his chair, lit a cigarette, and inhaled deeply before balancing it on the overflowing brass ashtray. He stirred his tea and took a loud slurp. The atmosphere was not normal, although what normal was I didn't quite know. As I tried to explain the sequence of events, I knew this would be the signal for trouble.

The alacrity with which he leapt up startled me, his narrow eyes transfixed as he studied the envelope with suspicion. He refused to open it.

'I've had one too,' I told him, hoping it would ease matters.

'Get rid of it,' he ordered as he undid the top button of his shirt. I glared at him in amazement.

'Don't you want to read it?' It seemed odd: me, his daughter talking to him like that. I was on my guard as I tried to gauge his reaction. It was obvious he could see my distress because he was not as wild as I had anticipated. This was remarkable self control for my father.

He flopped back into his creaking armchair. I studied him as his fingers drummed rhythmically on the arm. He still had not taken his eyes off the letter; I think he knew what it was about. Without warning he grabbed it, processed the first few lines then hurled the envelope onto the coffee table, the same hideous tiled table with pictures of vintage cars that Nancy had given us eight years ago.

He sat in silence. 'Didn't I know she'd be doing something foolish? Daffy thing!'

I perched on the arm of the settee to steady my wobbly legs.

I could hear Connie in the kitchen; she'd closed the door and was banging the crockery, no doubt anxious to block out our dialogue. Of course, she would. It was the safest place knowing this whole ghastly situation was of her making.

'*And* Mum's cleared her wardrobe,' I told him. 'She says she's been at her wits end.' I thought back to the storm it had caused the last time I defended my mother.

An awkwardness filled the air. When he left the room for a breather, I took a quick look to see what my mother had written:

> 'I'm writing to tell you that I have decided not to return home to you at the completion of my present stay with Mother.
>
> This decision has not been easy for me to take but I honestly feel that because of your attitude towards me it is the only possible choice open to me if I am to avoid a complete mental breakdown.
>
> I have always tried my best to please you, even to suffer for the sake of my daughter, the personal humiliation enforced upon me over the years. I cannot now however continue to bear the callous indifference you openly express to my endeavour and I have concluded that it would be best for me to spend the remaining years of my life away from this ever present, unhappy situation.
>
> In truth I am afraid of you and have not the strength to endure this existence any longer. Although I have not much strength, I still have my pride. I see loneliness ahead of me and there will probably be many other uncertainties, but I would rather face these than continue to suffer each day your obvious inhuman indifference to me as a person.
>
> I cannot forgive nor remain oblivious to your recent unreasonable attack upon me when you told me to leave you and take a furnished flat somewhere – anywhere.
>
> Indeed, your very attitude to me since this incident has worsened and I am in no doubt that it has been deliberately engendered to force me to take this drastic step.
> Blanche'

My mother had let it all pour out. It hit me just how unhappy this remarkable lady must have been.

Thrown into a world of helplessness and despair it was purgatory sitting at the dinner table that evening. Sick with worry I fled upstairs. Anxious to offload my devastating news, later that evening I rang Chris. 'And looks like she's gone for good,' I said, spluttering down the phone.

'I know. I've been waiting for your call.'

'You *what*!'

'When I visited just after your birthday, your mother took me on one side and explained what she'd be doing, only out of your earshot. Had a long chat with me she did. I was shocked, you can imagine. I'd no idea things were so bad between your parents. She put me in the picture about how unhappy she had been. For years she said.'

It was unreal to hear Chris talking to me about my own mother. 'And then she told me how she'd struggled with Connie being part of the family and how desperate she was to leave and free herself from the intolerable situation. She said she felt imprisoned but that she'd only put up with things for your sake until she knew you'd be getting married and have someone to support you.' I clutched my head as I listened. 'She explained how she'd been planning her escape for some time but knew she would have to judge her exit with caution.'

'Well, she never breathed a word to me.'

'She asked me to look after you. And, she made me promise not to say a word. Not to you. Not to anyone. But she didn't say when all this would be happening. I'd no idea so I've had to be on my guard just in case I said something I might regret.'

How on earth could she let Chris in on her plans and not confide in me? It didn't make sense.

'But why *you* and not me?'

'Said you'd be trying to stop her if she'd said anything. Like you did when she tried to escape in Saltford. I'm on my way,' Chris said. 'Can't see you upset like this.'

I envied him for his perfect childhood with a normal upbringing in a normal family home with normal parents who had no idea what an argument was. Doris and Bill had a millpond marriage, still living in their 1930s terraced house in Odd Down which they'd bought when they were first married. Chris's father put all his energies into following his son's passion for football and cricket and with Hampset cricket ground on their doorstep he supported him at every match. With a mother every bit as practical as mine, a seamstress who had served her apprenticeship at Jolly's in Bath, she was on a par with my mother when it came to those sumptuous homemade fruit cakes. Real gems, the pair of them, and if Chris had inherited his parents' supportive ways, then I knew I had struck lucky.

Fortunately, my mother approved of him from day one. And that went for my father, too, when I'd first brought him home one frosty evening whilst living in Saltford when icy conditions had made it impossible for his father's Austin to negotiate our steep turning. I felt nothing but relief when my mother sang his praises the following day.

The more I thought about it, the more I began to understand the logic behind my mother leaving. Once she sensed my relationship with Chris was serious, now, at the age of fifty-two, she would be able to build a new future for herself. Up to that point, it was something she could only dream about. And then I began to mull things over. Was she leaving to be with Howard? Selfishly, I had hoped their friendship might finish once we moved to Sea Mills but perhaps I was wrong and there was something going on about which I knew nothing.

Although I agonised over her leaving, I could never blame her. All I could do was thank her for remaining by my side during her traumatic marriage. My collapsed world had hit me in a way I had not thought possible but I had to realize this was the emancipation she both craved and deserved, and for her sake, I would have to put selfishness to one side and view her escape through adult eyes. With hindsight, I should have encouraged her to leave years before and begged her to take me with her we could both have had a better life. For her it was the start of a fresh beginning and an independence money could not buy.

It wasn't my life. Mine, thank goodness, was about to begin.

I felt tempted to ring the office the following morning with an excuse I was ill, but I was too conscientious for that. With my mind all over the place, I bashed away at my Olivetti typewriter and at dinner that evening I almost choked when Connie suggested that we both write to my mother.

'See if we can persuade her to rethink.' Rethink? Was she mad? I held back my mirth. I gave Connie my mother's letter to read so she could see for herself how troubled she had been. She tried to convince me that by writing we could get her back, but I knew otherwise. It was ludicrous for her to assume my mother would want to come crawling back to the misery she had endured for decades, when she had finally mustered up the courage to flee.

Nevertheless, that was what Connie did. And she made me write too.

Through tears and shock I cobbled together a letter; although Connie was persistent I should beg my mother to return, I wrote mine on the pretext of letting her know how much I loved her and I told her that once my father digested his letter he disappeared upstairs to his bedroom. I heard him blowing his nose, proof he was upset. Never had I known him let his bravado down. 'I'm afraid I have difficulty showing my feelings,' he explained later that evening. For him to admit to it was like being at confession, not that I had ever sat in one of those booths to ask for forgiveness, but it was how I imagined it. 'I can't help what I say and don't really mean it. One simply can't change their nature and curb their temper if that's how they're made.' I felt a duty to tell my mother exactly what he had said. He also pointed out, 'Now your mother's gone, Connie will have to go and live at her auntie Bill's.' She was an elderly friend from way back.

I flung him a venomous glance. 'Why now? I don't understand. Why's it only now you think she should move out?' My urge to challenge him surprised me but my frustration was bubbling.

'Awkward,' he went on, 'you know, living in the same house together.'

Well that's tough. Too bloody late, I thought. My mother must have felt sick when she digested the contents of my letter.

'And another thing, if your mother doesn't return soon, I'll start divorce proceedings on the grounds of desertion. I'm not having a wife who doesn't live with me.' I told her that he said he was going to give her a couple of days grace! My father's comments that Connie would have to move elsewhere were baffling. I visualised my mother screaming 'bloody marvellous'. A divorce was what she had hankered after for years. I also wrote saying that I hadn't realized things had got on top of her to such an extent but that I admired her for what she'd done. I finished by telling her I was missing her more than words could say, that I loved her and that she was to take care of herself.

Connie's letter, on the other hand, involved me. She made out *I* was the reason my mother should not have left:

'31st May 1970

My dear Blanche,

Naturally 'Hawk-Eye' [that's how Connie always referred to me] spotted something amiss straight away. Diane was in such a state I could hardly make out what was wrong at first and then could not believe it but she produced such evidence that I was forced to read in the end.

I beg of you do please come back. Poor Diane is heartbroken and is being so brave about it in an effort to keep things as normal as possible that it tears me apart to witness it.

Please don't do this to her, she is so insecure as it is, I don't think she would ever get over it. We are both shattered to think that you have been so unhappy that it has brought you to this drastic step but please change your mind before it is too late and we will try to work something out to make your life more palatable. At least give her a bit more time until she has married and has a home of her own and then she will at least have an anchor.

And have you thought of her wedding which can't be too distant? You know how she would feel about it if her parents were estranged. It would spoil everything for her. I don't think it would be fair to do this to her. After all, it isn't as if she has never bothered with you or about you, you know she is devoted to you and will miss you dreadfully. I know you must have thought about it beforehand, but you can't see her now and, if you could, I am sure you would be on your way back to comfort her.

I wish I could talk to you. I know you must have many just and valid arguments on your side but surely nothing can justify making someone you are responsible for, dreadfully unhappy?

I realize you must be unhappy too, but it can't be right to make the innocent and most vulnerable person suffer. We have lived three quarters of our lives and accept that a lot of it is unhappiness – who knows there may be a lot of it in store for Diane and it seems terribly cruel to create unhappiness which could be avoided.

I just don't know how to make my appeal strong enough,
but I do earnestly beg of you to give us another chance. We
are under great strain now and just hope and pray for good
news.
Love Connie'

What a cheek to say I beg of you to give *us* another chance. What
was all that about? And then the bitter twist of trying to put the
guilt on my mother by pointing out I was insecure. Was I? It was
obvious I was upset. What child wouldn't be? But making out I
was insecure; how on earth was I behaving? It was ludicrous. I
bristled at its contents and found the psychology behind it intriguing. And when had Connie ever been unhappy? She never
came anywhere near it. She was head strong and hard. Couldn't
she see she was the cause for my mother's deteriorating health?
She'd had enough of being a domestic slave to keep the place
spick and span; house chores were never on Connie's radar.

Considering her perceptive nature, it didn't make sense for
her to say she hadn't realized my mother had been unhappy; it
was obvious she'd have been aware of her long-term anxiety but,
it would seem, preferred to turn a blind eye.

But whatever promises she made on paper they were not the
promises my mother had hoped for. She didn't want to hear
Connie say they would try and work things out. She wanted her
out of the house, to which the letter made no reference.

I began to give up all hope of hearing from her. That was
until I received a phone call at work two days later.

'Darling. I need you to know I'm okay. I'm in a bedsit in
Bath.'

'Mum!' I choked at the sound of her voice. 'Are you …'

'I'm fine. Please don't be upset. You know how much I love
you.' I wanted to talk but couldn't find the right words. With her
suggestion that we speak later that evening, I bolted my dinner
and with a handful of shillings rushed to the public phone box on
the green at the end of our road. I felt comforted and reassured
the second I heard my mother's voice. 'How about we meet up
this coming Saturday in Bath?' she suggested. 'We can unwind
and have time together.'

Saturday could not come soon enough. In the meantime, I

tried to unravel my thoughts and feelings.

The second I spied my mother I ran the last few yards and fell into her arms.

'Forgive me, darling,' she begged. '*Please* forgive me. I hope you can understand. I've been longing to say it to you in person.'

'Mum. It's okay. You've nothing to apologise for.'

'I feel a lot better than a week ago. Honestly, if I hadn't got out when I did, I think I'd have gone mad. I'd come to the end of my tether. I couldn't take any more. Forgive …'

I interrupted her. 'Mum. I don't want you to feel guilty. Please.'

'I've tolerated that woman in the house since you were three. I think I deserve a medal.'

'But why didn't you tell me you were leaving?'

'I couldn't. And if your father had found out he'd have prevented me going I know.' She explained that it was to spare me the trauma, but the alternative was just as bad, if not worse. 'I didn't want it to turn out this way but when I knew you'd found Chris I felt it was the right time.' Her apologies came pouring out. 'And Linda, bless her … she was a star. Knowing your father would be at work she arrived early, cramming what belongings we could into her little Hillman Imp. I couldn't get out quick enough for fear he'd pop home for some reason. And poor Linda was terrified driving through Bristol, I remember. And have you seen this?' My mother delved in her handbag and flung Connie's creased letter across the table.

'Damn cheek. I wept when I read it… to think she was blaming me.' I squeezed her hands to offer comfort.

'I'm alright,' she reassured me. 'It'll take time but at least I'm free.'

Over the next couple of weeks calm prevailed at Sea Mills. My father even admitted he never thought my mother capable of doing such a thing. I wanted to tell him that he had only himself to blame but kept my thoughts to myself.

I picked up the threads of my daily routine and tried to put all my energies into my forthcoming wedding but without my mother's support there were times when I struggled to muster enthusiasm.

With an invitation from Chris's mother to join their family at weekends my father seemed to accept that I would often be away; it was a perfect opportunity to visit my mother and accompany Chris to cricket matches. And I was off to see them the following weekend.

With a promise from Chris to take me to a Berni steak house the following Saturday, I had been sitting in the lounge at Sea Mills finishing a lime green shift dress in readiness. All that remained was to pin the hem before retiring to bed but as I got up to clear away the coffee mugs my father caught me by surprise. We were alone, the mood silent except for the occasional sucking noise to keep his pipe alight.

He cleared his throat. 'Diane. Hang on.' He scratched his chin. 'I've been thinking. I'd um … I'd like to meet up with your mother. Like to … er … see her. So, I can, you know, talk to her about her stupidity.' He grimaced as he delivered his request. 'And as soon as possible. Within the next couple of days? See what you can arrange, there's a good girl.'

My stomach somersaulted. That would be Thursday by my reckoning.

My mother had been gone three weeks and my father was requesting a meeting. It was outrageous. Hadn't he got the message? Their marriage had gone beyond reconciliation. My mother knew it. I knew it. So how come my father didn't know it?

'It's ridiculous her going like this,' he said, his slipper tapping on the carpet.

With his Goliath temper, it was one hefty demand that I knew would spell alarm. The prospect of this so-called meeting filled me with horror. And where would the rendezvous take place? This tête-a-tête he thought my mother would be willing to join him for.

It was going to be a tricky encounter but first my mother would have to agree to it. And this Thursday … so soon!

I had to pick my time to ring her, but not before my father was out of the way.

'Wants *what*?'

My voice croaked as I delivered the request. 'I know Mum. I'm sorry.'

'Now listen. I don't want any further involvement with your

father. I'm worn out' she said, the thought of another battle unbearable.

'Says he merely wants to have a chat.'

'I bet! Look, I've made a clean break and he's got to understand that. Why after reading my letter would he think I would want to see him? And as for talking to him … he'll only be difficult. I don't feel I've got the strength for another show down. I know exactly what'll happen. And you do.'

The silence the other end of the phone said it all.

The following morning my phone rang at work. I glanced up at the clock on the office wall. It was ten thirty-two.

'Mum?'

'Look …' She sighed. 'Tell him I'll see him if I *must* … in Bath's Victoria Park. I just want to put a closure on this. And I hope he'll realize there's no going back. The way he's treated me and the indifference he's shown me, he's as good as told me to bugger off.'

Wary of his reactions and mood swings, I could not believe she had relented. But she would see him on one condition. And that condition involved me.

'I know it's not fair involving you darling, but I really don't think I can face him on my own.'

It was brave of my mother to agree to a meeting and I tried to think of a justified reason not to be present but there was no way I could let her down. I was twenty-one, an adult for God sake. This was just another of those torrid situations where she needed my support. My mind went into overdrive. The thought of telling my father she would only meet him if I could come along made me feel sick.

'Can't think why,' he snorted, rubbing the back of his neck in contemplation. 'What difference is it going to make?'

I knew full well why she wanted me there. 'I'm to be there otherwise there's no meeting.'

'Well, if that's what she wants, then come,' he said, opening his library book where he'd left off.

I was on edge and sleep would not come that night. Mary, my work colleague, wanted to know what the problem was. 'You look washed out,' she said. When my mother left home, Mary had been my life saver. Whisking me away from the office at lunchtimes to the nearby Bristol Downs, she parked her red Ford Escort where we took in the sights of the Clifton Suspension Bridge and ate black grapes picked fresh that morning from her vine.

Thursday dawned. The dullness of the day matched my feelings. I'd been to work as usual, but everything was a blur. I had no idea what to expect but there was one thing I did know, the meeting between my parents was going to happen.

Dinner that evening was a quiet affair. I had no appetite, chewing on imaginary mouthfuls of food. Even the dog seemed out of sorts; relieving himself of wind that called for a gas mask helped diffuse the tension.

The minute we finished our meal, my father was in the car revving the engine. He appeared keener than me to make a start. I dreaded what lay ahead but tried to bottle up my feelings. He chatted non-stop during our journey to Bath; I could tell he was taking things in his stride. As we approached, he checked the exact time of our meeting. He threw his dog-end out of the window and promptly lit another Peter Stuyvesant from the packet on top of the dashboard.

'Seven,' I told him.

'Only I want to be on time.' I felt sure my mother was praying he would not arrive.

Within spitting distance of the park, I braced myself for the show-down between them. I was about to witness my mother and father coming together for a farcical meeting. It seemed crazy. How on earth had it got to this? I'd never heard of my friends embroiled in such goings on so why the hell *me*?

As we drove through the impressive wrought iron gates into a quieter than normal Queen's Avenue, my father readjusted himself in his seat. We cruised, his eyes swinging from left to right as he tried to locate my mother. Through a haze of drizzle, I spotted her in the distance the second we drove in. In her flat black shoes and a Marks and Spencer's hounds-tooth raincoat she looked a lonely figure.

'There she is!' he said. 'Daffy thing.' He sped the last few yards and pulled up alongside her with a jerk.

He had wound his window down in readiness. 'Fancy a cuppa?' he asked through the cigarette fug, as though hoping for a social get together. Cuppa? I'd never known him take my mother for a cuppa, as he put it, in his life. It wasn't something he did and, if he had taken her, it would never have been just the two of them.

'Car's fine.' My mother had a conviction in her voice.

I leapt out and as I threw my arms around her saw a ghostly grey face screwed up with anguish. I'd seen it before. My father, on the other hand, appeared relaxed as though all would be well. I feel sure he had no intention of rocking the boat.

'So, Blanche, how are you?' There was a tenderness in his voice I don't ever recall hearing.

'Well, Mother's not well.' Grandma was unwell but I had not breathed a word. I could not believe she'd dared to drop her name into the conversation. It was fuel for the fire, always had been, knowing my father had never hit it off with his mother-in-law. I could never understand why it always struck such a raw nerve with him whenever her name cropped up. She was a sweet-ie; old before her time with a warmth and gentleness that made her special.

'Sorry to hear that.' I wondered whether this was genuine compassion or just an act.

My heart was thumping at twice its normal rate.

'Now what's all this about?'

'Vic, I *cannot* go on living the way I have, and you can't expect me to continue doing so. I have made sacrifices on every front and tried to live with things the way they are. Besides, my health's suffering. You must surely know that. Enough is enough.'

Blimey. It didn't sound like my mother. It was like a role reversal; my father with a caring approach and my mother with a forthrightness I had not witnessed before.

Loud shrieks punctuated the air from a group of lads playing football over by the bandstand. I was envious there were people out there having fun and I hoped to goodness the couple walking past had not heard my mother tell my father how selfish he was, never once sparing a thought for her.

I tried to think of something appropriate to say, a little pleas-antry to throw in, anything to relieve the tension, but decided silence was best. My knees were trembling. I prayed the meeting would soon be over. My father suggested that my mother need

151

not work so many hours in the newsagents and even offered to do a bit more around the home, but she was not falling for his false promises.

Never had I heard them discuss these things. Whenever my mother tried to engage with him, he would tell her it was poppycock.

My father didn't talk about the real reason for my mother leaving and never once mentioned Connie. But it was too late for change now.

I hadn't needed to intervene thank God, but it was a black day. I knew it would be the last time we would all be together, just the three of us as I had longed for since infancy. While my gaze flitted from one parent to the other my childhood flashed before me. I wanted to bury my head in my hands and weep but knew that would not help matters.

They talked for a minute or two longer. I saw my father grimace in the knowledge his last-ditch attempt to win her back had failed.

'Right!' he said and before I knew it, we had left the park with my mother not given the opportunity to make her escape. Focused and determined, he hurtled along.

No-one said a word. My mother sat straight backed, her brow puckered as she stared out of her side window. I studied her, concerned for her well-being, knowing this was what she had feared. Almost five miles out of Bath, I leapt when my mother screamed:

'Stop the car! I'm about to be sick!'

My father rammed the brake to the floor and we almost shot through the windscreen.

She flung open her door and tumbled to the pavement.

My father's 'Bye, Blanche' tore me apart.

I felt helpless in the back of the car and prayed she had not injured herself. I ached to tell her I loved her, to take care of herself and to ring me as soon as she got back to that measly bedsit of hers, but there was no time for any of that. All I could do was blow her a couple of air kisses.

I watched my mother head off slowly in the opposite direction, and as my father pulled away with lightning speed, we travelled home in a car fuelled with anger.

It was at times like these I longed for a sibling but with no-one to turn to I would have to continue with the invisible battle I had learnt to cope with over the years. But not having to listen to any more arguments or watch my mother fall into a deeper trough of depression would be a relief.

Back at Sea Mills there were now just the three of us. But it was the wrong three. The thought of turning my back on a home that carried so many unhappy memories and ridding myself of the tainted Berry surname could not arrive soon enough.

But first, there was another hurdle to overcome.

Diane Harding

CHAPTER 16
THREE WEDDINGS AND TWO FUNERALS

Happiness was now within sight and the warmer days began to lift my spirits although hovering at the edge of my consciousness I worried, knowing my parents would once again be coming face to face on my wedding day. Just months away, it was an anxious time. I feared my father would misbehave but Chris tried his best to reassure me. I had lost trust in people after my mother left home but knew I would have to put my feelings to one side.

I took solace in my weekends away at his parents' home in Bath; it was an opportunity to focus on my future. But after returning from one of these visits, my father presented me with an agonising predicament. I was reclining on my bed engrossed in a letter from my mother telling me how she had enjoyed our outing to Stourhead the previous Saturday when I heard my father's car pull into the drive. It was normal for him to change out of his work clothes at the end of the day, but his heavy footsteps stopped outside my room. I put my hands together and prayed he would not come in.

'You in there, love?' I shoved the letter under my bed.

He entered and shouldered the door shut. 'I'm sorry angel,' he said, drawing air through his front teeth. 'I know it's not long before your wedding, but I won't … won't be able to give you away.'

'What do you mean, you won't be able to give me away?'

His Adam's apple bobbed up and down as he swallowed. 'I've been thinking about it and don't really feel I can do it. I'm sorry if you're upset.' He stood there and rubbed his bull-dog jaw.

'Upset?' That was the moment I hated my father. I don't know why I didn't leap up and slap his face, but I knew I'd come off worse. A silence like a graveyard in the dead of night hung over the room. Hot tears dripped as I stood there glaring at a face devoid of emotion. I had no idea what was going on in that brain of his. Why was he doing this to me? What had I done to deserve it? If I were his angel, then how the hell could he be so cruel? Had he spared a thought for his only daughter? Couldn't he see my wounds were still raw from my mother leaving home? We had even discussed walking down the aisle together, me on his right arm. Wasn't that what every father dreamed of? The mere thought of my parents meeting up was enough to fret about. It was hard to imagine how he could be so gutless. Was it because he could not face meeting his wife while a messy divorce was in progress or was the real reason because he would feel too embarrassed to meet the relations? Either way he was about to ruin the most important day of my life.

I slammed the door shut and leant against it for a second or two. The world was unfair. Life was unfair. I never knew what he was going to come out with next. It was as if he was not my father. As if we were strangers. I longed to reach out to him and feel his arms around me but all I could do was dream.

I reflected on his cowardly decision, knowing that this was someone who always wanted the best of everything, even suggesting Chris and I marry in Clifton Cathedral. Connie didn't appear uncomfortable knowing she would be attending the wedding; she'd already shown me her hat. I'd considered how my mother would react when she saw her sitting in the pew alongside other members of my family although I guess because she'd woven herself into the fabric of our daily lives everything would appear normal.

I kicked off my slippers and curled up on my bed. Could this day get any worse?

When I rang to tell Chris the news, he could not believe my

father could be so heartless. He said to attend his daughter's wedding was the least he could do. I was never sure what he thought of his future father-in-law and his antics, but I had a bloody good idea. I lay in bed that night pondering the implications of no father to give me away.

The following weekend, when the topic reared its head in front of Chris's parents and I saw Doris shake her head, I knew my father's reputation had hit rock bottom.

I debated who Chris and I could ask to do the honour; we were a family of few, but I'd had a brainwave. My loyal uncle Stan, my father's brother-in-law, would be the perfect candidate. Nancy and Stan were extremely fond of my mother and, knowing what she had endured over the years, Stan and my father had had their disagreements. As a young child, I recall a row between them over Connie, after which they did not speak for years. I felt sure he would hold up two fingers to him and gleefully agree to my request.

'That's typical of your father,' he said when I told him. 'He always was a selfish bugger. He only ever thought of himself.'

For weeks I lived with the uncertainty and gave my father the silent treatment. Whether he had noticed how his decision had infuriated me, his conscience must have pricked him.

After tending his allotment one evening and without warning, he said, 'Diane. I've been thinking. You know I'll be with you on your big day. It was foolish of me. I was only thinking of myself.' His attitude had changed, as though he had waved a magic wand. I wondered if Connie had intervened and told him not to be so childish. He seemed to listen to her advice. Or had guilt got the better of him? Or was it because he felt sorry for me?

As my wedding day approached, Chris's cosy home was where my mother and I shared memorable times. He insisted we visit her as often as we could; he hated the thought of her being alone in her cramped bedsit. But one July weekend, while I was colouring her hair, there was a ring on the doorbell. My mother leapt up, wrapped her head in a towel, patted her cheeks in the mirror and rushed downstairs. She was talking to someone.

'Listen!' I said, nudging Chris.

I heard laughter as they approached. And then the door edged open. It was Howard. My hand flew to my chest as a slow disbelieving smile began to emerge. He put out his hand to introduce himself, but I had of course met him initially at the bus stop a couple of years earlier when we lived in Saltford, though for Chris it was their first encounter. Of medium build with bushy eyebrows and a dark head of hair neatly parted to one side, Howard looked smart in a check jacket and tie. He displayed an engaging and lively personality, soon discussing with Chris his love of golf and the coincidence they both worked in the same Ministry establishment in Bath. After we left, Chris said he found him charming but admitted he worried about my reaction having him there.

Although I could tell my mother had found someone in whose company she appeared at ease, at the time I knew nothing of the secret romance that was evolving between them. To have my close relationship with her invaded, and her affection shared by another person, had its difficulties.

But there was little I could do. They were circumstances out of my control.

The day of our wedding was 21 August 1971. I woke early to overcast skies and the steady drum of rain on the window, but nothing could have dampened my spirits. My father was upbeat and on his best behaviour. He even delivered a gin and tonic to my bedroom before I left for the church. And for him to tell me that he was delighted for me made my heart pound.

Diane and Chris's wedding day, August 1971

In the line up for the photographs, my parents joined in the spirit of the occasion with my father oozing his usual charm as he shook hands with all the guests. The impressive wedding luncheon at the Avon Gorge Hotel and the panoramic views overlooking the Clifton Suspension Bridge were unforgettable moments.

Relocating to Southdown on the outskirts of Bath, I signed on with an agency to do temporary secretarial work and on that first morning skipped along to the offices of Morris' Estate Agents in the city centre. As well as the property side of the business, it was also my role to hold the fort every Wednesday while Mr Morris – Doc to all his farming buddies – performed his auctioneering duties at Bath Cattle Market, while Mr Wise, his able assistant, documented the sale and movement of livestock.

The offices were on the first floor with a display of glossy black and white photographs on the half landing showing recent property sales; to my amazement I saw my Saltford home, which my father had purchased prior to it going under the hammer.

What a coincidence, I thought.

Once I completed my temporary three weeks, I was delighted to accept the offer of a permanent position with the company. Finally, at the age of twenty-two, things were on a high. I had never had it so good and was the happiest I had ever been. I was in love with life and floating with joy.

That was until I took a phone call at work one afternoon.

I broke out in a sweat at the sound of my father's voice.

'Darling! Hello.'

My brain whirred into action.

'Dad, what's up?' He seldom rang me at work except once on a previous occasion to give me the gruesome details of how he had sliced off the top of his thumb on his circular saw. He explained that he had done a foolish thing. While switched on he had attempted to attach the safety guard and was off to hospital to see if they could stitch the thumb back. So, what the hell was this phone call about? 'You okay?'

There was a pause. I swallowed hard, anticipating the worst. 'Thought I'd ring you, darling, and let you know that I'm … I'm um … getting married.'

I gripped the black receiver for all I was worth. I had no idea what to think, so just listened. '*Married*?' This wasn't something that had ever crossed my mind. He was getting married. That's what he said.

'You … er … you know who to, don't you?' as though waiting for the answer to come from me. His voice faltered the other end of the phone as I digested his sudden news.

The silence between us was mutual. I felt like calling his bluff by asking whether it was Cassandra or Caroline? Or could it be a customer who called into his shop?

'Connie, I presume,' I said, struggling to muster enthusiasm.

I wasn't aware he knew any other female. I scraped my chair away from my desk across the hard lino floor.

'Correct!' he replied, as though relieved I'd come up with the right answer. My blood boiled as I sat pondering this rapid romance.

I tried to show my adult self-restraint but there was no way I could offer my congratulations. I wondered why he hadn't told me his news face to face when I'd seen him last but guessed he'd decided it better to ring so he couldn't see my reaction. Until that phone call he had never touched on the subject.

I banged the phone down, thankful everyone was out of the office. Things had happened so hastily; it wasn't long ago my mother had fled the family home, troubled, and tormented over the fact Connie was still living at Sea Mills and now she was marrying my father. All I could do was spare a thought for my long-suffering mother.

I was to inherit a stepmother. I didn't like the thought of it, and neither did I like the thought of another woman replacing my mother but that was something I had no control over. And then I began to wonder if my parents' marriage had been one of convenience for a myriad reasons, least of all so Connie could work in the business.

My father's call was quick, and our conversation stilted. Connie would not have to practise her new role as stepmother because she had been around since I was a little girl. I had grown up with her. I knew her and she knew me, my ways, my likes, my dislikes, what traits I had inherited from my mother, my father and I guess from her too.

I can still feel the gut-wrenching agony that the person my mother had so despised was to marry my father. The possibility of him remarrying had never occurred to me as I had never witnessed any outward sign of affection between them. For someone who never missed a thing, it was hard to imagine I'd had no whiff of suspicion; the only difference after their wedding was that my father had pushed together the two single beds in his room. Until that point, when my mother was still at home, a wooden varnished bedside table my father had made separated their beds.

As the weeks rolled by, my mother became a changed person; with her renewed freedom she was always beaming and, because of this, I decided I couldn't care less what went on back in Sea Mills. I made a point of never mentioning the place, but I began to consider my dilemma if she was to enquire about my father. Despite everything, she occasionally asked after him, although I could not think why. If she were to ask after him, or, worse still, whether Connie was still living in Sea Mills, I had a choice. Would I be honest and explain, at the risk of hurting her feelings even more, or would I say nothing? I thought I might have to tell a white lie but told myself I would have to deal with that when the moment arose.

As for my father, he would have to enlighten the neighbours; those nosy parkers whose gossip over the garden fence was an important part of their day. Surely, they would want to know why my mother had left without warning, not to mention the grilling he would receive from his customers in the shop. But thank goodness I would not have to be involved with any of that.

Not long after I had received that startling news my mother caught me off guard during one of our shopping excursions to Bath.

'Presume Connie's still at Sea Mills.' It startled me to hear her mention her name.

'Yip,' I responded. Without a second thought I continued to tell her, 'And getting married!' I don't know what made me divulge the hurtful information. I was furious for my naïve response.

My mother sniggered as the realization dawned. 'No wonder he couldn't wait to get the divorce through. Pity he wouldn't agree to it all those years ago and not waited for things to come to a head. We might have all had a life.' I could never understand why, when my mother left home, my father had said that Connie would have to live elsewhere. That was what my mother had longed for. All I hoped was that he hadn't kept my mother prisoner to safeguard his reputation. But, back then, even as a twenty-one-year-old, I was clueless; if only I had thought more then maybe I could have seen it. It seems crazy now, but it was true.

In the February of 1974, my father and Connie were married at Bristol Registry Office but not before another awkward phone call that sent my heart racing.

'Darling, I'd appreciate it if you and Chris could be witnesses.'

Oh my God. He had a nerve. Had he remembered the distress he'd caused when he told me he couldn't give me away at my own wedding? And now he was asking a giant favour. His request troubled me, and I pondered at length as to what I should do. I felt tempted to play him at his own game but like my mother, always the pleaser, with reluctance I agreed. That night I lay in bed and reflected on my stupidity.

Studying the pair of them in the Registry Office I could not get over the fact they had fallen for one another. With a pit in my stomach I wondered how long it had been going on and to think I had never sussed the situation was baffling. During the short ceremony I found myself gazing out of the window; I needed to do something to avert my attention. I nudged Chris and wondered what he might be thinking.

After the service, my father whisked us off for a luncheon to an old-world pub in the countryside. Neither Chris nor I were keen to go. In so many ways it was a poignant day and one in which Chris's suspicions that he had a violent allergy to prawns were confirmed!

Although my father had tied the knot within weeks of receiving his divorce papers, my mother and Howard's wedding would take another seventeen months; it wasn't until years later that I discovered my mother had been cited in Howard's divorce which had protracted the dissolution of his own marriage.

The date of my mother's and Howard's marriage was 17 July 1975. It was Connie's birthday, as it happened. I often wondered whether it was so my mother could stick her fingers in the air and tell her she too could do it, but she was too ladylike for any of that. After the ceremony in Cheltenham Registry Office, we celebrated the happy event at Freda and Frank's home nearby. Whereas I couldn't have cared less about my father remarrying, I was delighted to think my mother was carving out a new future for herself.

Blanche and Howard's wedding day, July 1975

Not only had I acquired a stepmother and a stepfather in a short space of time, but Howard's daughter, Gloria, five years older than me, meant I was gaining a stepsister. It took a while for these rapid changes in my life to sink in; circumstances I would have to adapt to over time.

In Chris's own words, 'his life was simple and uncomplicated'.

If only I could have said the same about mine.

When I was twenty-six, concerned I may have an eating disorder, I made an appointment to consult the doctor. I was unable to sleep, had lost my appetite and was losing weight. Although happily married with no worries, the medical verdict pointed to a possible delayed reaction from the trauma I had experienced over the years. I thought I had let go of my angst, but I was wrong. Events buried deep inside forced their way into my conscience all too often; the heightened stress levels I had lived through played a key role. I found difficulty in identifying with my past, a past mapped out from a tender age, and because I was powerless to let go, I had discovered a way to internalise information.

The Valium prescribed by my doctor I took under duress, but because it made me feel agitated with a sinking feeling of not belonging, I hurled the remainder in the bin. It felt wrong to depend on a pill for peace of mind and soon it became apparent that with Chris's encouragement, I was able to rebuild the tumbled framework of my life. I needed to prove to myself there was no way I was going to allow my past experiences to take hold of me.

After five years and with fond memories, I left the estate agents two weeks prior to the arrival of our son, Richard. During the hectic months that followed, my father and Connie would sometimes travel over to Bath to pay us a visit, but it was never for any length of time. The second he was through the door, he would announce that he couldn't stay long, as though he needed to forewarn me. Trying to persuade him was like battling against a strong current. It became a joke but one that infuriated me. The minute he had downed his cup of tea, he would start pacing. He was retired, so why wouldn't he want to spend time getting to know his adorable grandson, unlike Chris's parents who jumped at every opportunity. Chris could never understand him.

Connie did not have any relatives, except for Viv her older sister. Years after Viv's husband, Bill, died, she became ill herself with a decision taken for Connie to care for her in Sea Mills. What shocked me was to learn that my father had given Viv an ultimatum; she would not be welcome unless she altered her will. He thought she should leave her money to her sister and not to charity. Where were his feelings?

Two years later, Chris secured the next leg of his promotion. Eager to progress, he accepted the offer and although he would be working in Weymouth, we settled on a new property in the nearby market town of Dorchester. Although it was goodbye to Chris's parents in Bath, this move was to my advantage; we were only eight miles from my mother and Howard who had settled in the picturesque village of Upwey.

Soon after moving, our daughter, Emma, arrived making our family unit complete, with a determination on my part to bring up my children in as normal and uncomplicated an environment as possible. I would see to it that nothing would ever come between us. Ever.

Weekends were special. With damp sand crunching between our toes and squawking seagulls soaring and tumbling overhead we spent Saturday mornings on Weymouth's deserted beach, our daughter digging for gold and our son testing out the racing cars sculpted by his father; it was the quietest time, when holiday makers had vacated their bed and breakfast and new arrivals had yet to descend.

I also remember with fondness the outings with my stepsister, Gloria, and husband, Brian. With their family of three and my two and a blustery sea breeze blowing through our hair, we talked, laughed, and hiked our way along the steep rugged coastal path at Bowleaze Cove at the opposite end of Weymouth's long stretch of golden sand. Another favourite jaunt was trudging up Maiden Castle in Dorchester, a fortified Iron Age hill-top settlement. The boisterous youngsters revelled in the freedom; to scramble up the steep embankments and dodge the roaming cows provided epic thrills. An embarrassing memory was when the grazing cows gave chase and how my first reaction was to drop the buggy, leap the stile and flee, leaving the others to fend for themselves. Although we still laugh about that shameful incident, it's a moment I don't care to think about.

Another promotion in 1983 had us retracing our steps back to Bath, this time to a property in Saltford, the village I moved to with a heavy heart in 1966. Only this time, it was different. With excitement and eagerness, we were returning to once more be nearer Chris's parents.

Soon after our arrival, with friends and what family members we could muster together, we arranged a surprise party for Doris and Bill's Golden Wedding, but Chris's father was unwell; with a diagnosis of emphysema his breathing had become problematic. Sadly, the following year, Bill died with the discovery that the dreadful disease was the result of exposure to the asbestos he had worked with all his life as a carpenter. It was a significant loss; he was the first of our parents to die. He was a wonderful man and I often wished I'd had a father as devoted as Chris's father had been to his son.

Although my father was never one for holidaying abroad, for

whatever reason, he and Connie had become infatuated with Turkey. There was something about the place that resonated with them but returning home from one of these visits he had developed a persistent cough. I had grown up with his coughing bouts, so it did not strike me as unusual. Repeated hospital appointments showed no diagnoses until he attended a physiotherapy appointment for a painful neck.

'It's shocking news.' Connie cleared her throat. 'They've … found lumps.'

'Oh?' I croaked.

'It's inoperable. Lung as Dad thought.'

'Why can't they … '

'Nothing they can do. Spread to his other organs. He's asked me to tell you. Said he couldn't face it.'

I stood with my back propped against the hall wall, the phone gripped in my sweaty palm. For years, I'd lectured my father that if he gave up smoking it would help to prolong his life but he'd brush it aside pointing out that he had no other vices so he might as well enjoy himself.

I had a visceral urge to see him. I needed time with him. To talk to him. To look him in the eye and hear him explain the reason for his intolerable behaviour towards my mother and why he had allowed Connie to become part of my family. Although every visit to Sea Mills conjured up a nightmare sensation if I wanted answers, I would have to steel myself.

'He's taken it badly,' Connie whispered the second I stepped inside. 'He's just popped into the garden for a bit of fresh air.'

I rushed to the lounge window. My father was still in his pyjamas, standing half-way down the paved path, motionless, his head tilted to one side as though studying the fruits of his labour. Images of a once handsome Roger Moore lookalike flashed before me. But all that had vanished. His silhouette shocked me. He turned around and shuffled back towards the house, slow and stooped. I thought his pathetic sight might have produced a twinge of sadness, but I felt nothing.

We sat and sipped tea together in the front room, his hands wrapped round his cup, his eyes cast downwards.

He then looked over to me. 'Diane,' he said. 'I haven't mentioned this to you before.' He struggled to get his breath, 'but I'm leaving you a little more money in my will than I'd originally planned.' He leaned forward on his elbows. 'Connie will need somewhere to live so I've left her the house.' I could not find the correct words to respond. All I could do was stare at him. Did he think a little extra money would compensate for the past; for his mood swings and for the troubled times I had lived through? Or was this his way of apologising for allowing another person to dislocate my upbringing? Whatever it was, no amount of money could make amends. It was too late for that.

It was to be my father's seventy-first birthday in a couple of days so I left his present on the sideboard in readiness: the comfy soft topped socks were the only thing Connie suggested he could do with.

I sat and thought about the questions I needed answering and, judging by his frailty, I knew I would have to act fast. To see his head buried in his hands it hit me that I would not have a father much longer. Although he still displayed a youthfulness with his dark head of hair and little sign of facial wrinkles, it was obvious he was suffering, so I thought it best to leave my interrogation until I called the following weekend.

I rose early on the Saturday and drove over to Bristol with high hopes. The scenario of our meeting had played over in my head throughout the week and during the half hour journey I thought of nothing else.

I stood on the doorstep, paused for a moment, then tapped the knocker. My heart raced and I had that same familiar dryness in my mouth. I told myself not to be ridiculous. I was the one that had chosen to see him again but as I entered the hall the smell of illness caught in my throat. To learn from Connie that my father's bed was now downstairs in the dining room alarmed me.

'Gone downhill rapidly' she explained as I stood outside the door unsure whether to knock before entering. 'Go on in,' she gestured. 'He knows you're coming.'

'I need to talk to him,' I told her in soft tones.

Connie raised her eyebrows. 'Not sure he's up to it.'

I opened the door a fraction. With half-drawn curtains, enough light shafted through to see an emaciated skeleton propped up on plumped pillows. I tried not to show surprise. He moved his bony hand across his chest, the thin papery skin covered in blue and purple patches. He attempted to turn his head.

'Hello darling,' he mouthed. To enquire how he was feeling seemed inappropriate, so I focussed my attention on his grandchildren. I didn't expect him to answer so I did all the talking.

It was hard to comprehend that this person I was studying was my father; that special daddy who would sit me on his lap as a young child and sing me lullabies. I thought about his endearing letters written to my mother after he had first set foot in Cape Town and her eagerness to receive news from her 'Vicky' as she referred to him. It was both comforting and heart-warming to know he had once felt deep affection towards her and that I was the product of their love.

I jumped as Connie poked her head round the door. She crept over to my father and held out a baby's feeding cup from which he took a sip of water. And then he mumbled something from his parched lips. I couldn't make it out. I wondered if he were attempting to explain his stupidity but knew he would never admit to any wrongdoing. I felt tempted to ask him to repeat it but there seemed little point. I stood at his bedside, biting my bottom lip, my head reminding me why I had come but my heart telling me not to confront this dying man. It was my final chance to speak to him but, given the circumstances, I realized that my questions were now of little consequence. I had left it too late.

I touched his arm before giving him one last kiss. His eyes flickered. 'Love you darling,' he murmured.

'Love you too,' I replied, knowing this would be the last time I would see him.

I left the house wildly frustrated by my cowardliness and the probing I had intended to do. I had missed my opportunity and with nothing resolved had only myself to blame. I had let myself and future generations down.

I drove home in a daze, the old proverb playing over in my mind about never put off till tomorrow what you can do today. It made me appreciate how important it is to have a close relationship with a father, something I had never experienced.

Four days after my visit in the June of 1989 my father died.

Connie rang me in the early hours of the morning to tell me she had intended to stay awake, but she had dozed off and seconds later, 'he'd gone'. Her emotions were in control as she relayed the news. I had never once seen her cry. Neither of us offered one another our condolences; I would have remembered if we had. Tears trickled but they were not for the father I had lost, but for the father I felt I never knew.

When my mother first heard of his ill health, she requested regular bulletins. With news of his death, she told me she would like to attend his funeral and made me promise to let her know when details had been finalised. Her gracious reaction staggered me, but she was adamant. The message on her flowers read, 'So many memories.' Her poignant words were as though she bore no grudge.

After a marriage that spanned fifteen years Connie was now a free woman and, in the year following my father's death, she made the decision to put down new roots in Southport. When the dormer bungalow opposite her lifelong friend, Freda, came on the market she wasted no time in making an offer.

The following year gave us another wrench. With Chris away in the States on business, I received news that his mother had suffered a stroke. Not wishing to disrupt his trip I decided to say nothing until his return but in his absence the children and I visited Doris every day in hospital to keep up her spirits. A week later, still smelling of her Pond's cream, she returned home. Although her cuddly nature remained intact her speech caused problems; males became females, rights became lefts and ups became downs. She was an inspiration to anyone who knew her; she managed her confusion in a positive way and would have us all in stitches with her infectious laughter.

The four years that followed were hectic with 1994 a bitter-sweet time for us as a family.

CHAPTER 17
CHRISTMAS IN CAPE TOWN

Although in 1994 we mourned the death of Doris after a severe and unexpected heart attack, Chris and I knew she would have wanted us to continue with our plans for what for him would be his first trip to Cape Town and for me a momentous return to my roots. Having heard me talk so much about this idyllic country, I was keen to show my family where I had spent the first fourteen years of my life. It was a journey I was determined to make and, despite the difficulties during my early years, it is still the place I call home.

I was nervous at what I might find and curious as to whether I would see things in a different light but I could not let the intrusion of negative memories impact on my visit nor allow the pain of recalled events to show in my face; for the sake of my family I would have to adopt my pretend-it-never-happened attitude.

Being a Bathonian, Chris had recently had a reunion with friends from his youth. To visit old haunts where once he had roamed as a child and stand outside the house where he had grown up to me seemed unimaginable. The only person I have reconnected with from my past is Jenny from Cape Town. Although she now lives in Tunbridge Wells, every Christmas we do our annual reminiscing by telephone, me keen to find out whether she has been in contact with Beverley Ellis, who back in 1963 was on our boat en route for a holiday to England, or Carole Redford who shared my passion for mint imperials and whose mother was a tall, slinky model.

We booked our flight to coincide with the school holidays in the December of that year and as our South African Airways 747 roared into the skies above Heathrow on that Thursday, my stomach churned with a cocktail of emotions. On the screen ahead of me, I monitored our steady climb into the heavens and within minutes gladly accepted a glass of wine which, in my excitement, I promptly spilt over the lady to my left.

Far too excited to sleep, thirteen hours later I watched the vast expanse of metal wing gently oscillating under a bright cloudless sky and as we reduced power and prepared for our descent, the awesomeness of Table Mountain loomed like a prehistoric monster. And when I heard the wheels of our jumbo screech as they struck the tarmac at D F Malan airport, I knew I was back. My diary entry read:

> 'Emerged from the plane and collided with sweltering heat.'

We negotiated our hired automatic Toyota Camry out of the airport, our two in the back staggered we'd been able to keep a secret that it wasn't the Volkswagen Jetta we'd had so much fun teasing them about. They informed their father there was no 'cred' with a car like that.

Just seconds into our journey I was shocked and saddened to discover that the non-white squatter camps were still a sea of slums, just as overcrowded as I had remembered them. Nothing had changed in the thirty-one years since I had left, their compound still littered with fragile, make-shift wooden and corrugated shacks with the gap between rich and poor as wide as ever.

I was intrigued to know if dormant memories would come flooding back as I trod the fiendishly hot pavements of this dynamic city and if strolling along palm-fronted beaches and visiting familiar surroundings would feel and smell the same. I was also impatient to immerse myself in the culture and the language; that strong South African accent my father was determined I was never to inherit and to savour the atmosphere and exotic fruits that had once seemed commonplace.

As we checked into our first stop at the Vineyards Hotel in

Newlands, the place where Jenny's mother had so often taken me for Sunday lunch, my overload of nostalgia was almost too much to handle. Everything seemed more magical than I had remembered. The same flag-stoned flooring welcomed us into the entrance lobby and vivid magenta bougainvillea with its delicate papery flowers hung in profusion from the pergola at the rear of the building. As the mighty spectacle of Table Mountain stared down on us, I was delighted to catch a glimpse of a Cape Sugarbird with its long slender tail feathers and the evening when the heavens opened I drank in the sweet smell of rain beating down on parched terraces. My stay would not have been complete without ordering Bobotie from the menu, a well-known South African dish made from spiced minced lamb with an egg-based topping, which I adored. My diary the next day read:

'In bed all day with food poisoning. Must have been the Bobotie!!'

I tried to stagger down to the pool with the family the following morning, but weakness forced me to retreat to my bed for the remainder of the day. Despite this set-back, I was determined to sample the delicious Snoek fish with its naturally salty flavour.

It alarmed me to discover that there were buildings no longer standing; fallen victim to regeneration, state-of-the-art complexes made areas unrecognisable. I also had difficulty identifying with the docks where, all those years ago as I departed its shores for England, Jenny stood at the quayside with her family and held on to the streamers I threw over the side of the ship. Now the Victoria and Albert Waterfront, it is one of the main vibrant attractions in the heart of Cape Town's working harbour.

A poignant visit was to Herschel, the school my father always reminded me was costing him a fortune. With an appointment to look round, an enthusiastic caretaker greeted us the minute we arrived. Sir William Herschel with his bronze bust still in situ welcomed us and, built after I had left, the archive room lined with class photographs kick-started my nostalgia. I shrieked to see myself as an innocent eight-year-old in 1957, sitting cross-legged in the front row of a black and white picture. We wandered the dormitories where I'd agonised for the boarders unable to visit their parents at weekends and then the playing fields, a little smaller than I'd remembered, where I'd taken part in hockey matches and the tennis practice wall my father had contributed towards financially all those years ago. As though time had stood still, I breathed in the same smell in the dining room. It brought a smile to my face to see the original pictures still adorning the walls and I shuddered as I entered the hall where Miss Louw took us for gym. With her light blue aertex shirt and navy shorts, her watchful eye followed us as she put us through the rigours of rope climbing and vaulting over boxes in our tee shirts and voluminous blue elasticised knickers. I had inherited my mother's petite figure and, being the shortest in my class, I remember everyone cheered the day she weighed and measured us and, at fourteen, I had finally reached five feet.

My diary entry reminded me:

'New Year's Eve saw Buddy Holly performance at theatre. Coffee and port in our bedroom afterwards. Toured Cape Town Castle. Nearly fried in surrounding courtyard.'

We left Cape Town behind to travel the forty minutes through dramatic valleys remote of urban life and rolling hills blanketed with the region's unique fynbos and when I spied the sign for Franschhoek I was back at Excelsior Farm where my mother and I spent happy holidays in the hope it would help repair her frayed nerves. And then I had a flashback and saw Connie diving into the swimming pool and insisting I perform a poem at the talent contest. Even away from the confines of home, it seemed my mother could never escape her presence.

Determined to maximise our time, it was off to Stellenbosch, the famous wine region with its acres of impressive fertile fields swathed in orderly vineyards that stretched as far as the eye could see. It was the highlight for my teenagers who were eager to tour the wineries and impatient to sample the liquid delights that followed.

We felt spoilt for choice with vast stretches of beaches and hidden coves. Under a blazing hot sun, we spent Christmas morning soaking up the atmosphere on the secluded Dalebrook beach before returning to the hotel for a festive celebration. Later that afternoon, we huddled round the phone to send good wishes to my mother who was spending Christmas with Howard at his daughter's home in Bath. Talking to her six thousand miles away, her voice crackled with emotion before she burst into tears. I agonised for her and presumed powerful memories had come scuttling back.

The thrill of immersing myself in the forgotten splendour of the place and the endless sun-baked road I had travelled along to Gordon's Bay as a child still provided that same surge of joy.

I was back, me in my ruched swimming costume, my fair hair encased in a white strap-fastened-under-the-chin swimming cap, happy and contented. What saddened me was my discovery that the quaint, white-washed church where its black congregation sang their hearts out every Sunday, had disappeared.

It was hard to believe that everything that was once was no more. New shops and apartments had sprung up, the only thing the same was the blistering sun, the crunchy sand, the sniff of the ocean and the continual roar of the waves crashing against gigantic sun-warmed boulders, ebbing and flowing on the shoreline that left a residue of filigree spray just as it had done all those years ago. This was where we hung out from early morning until our shadows became elongated outlines in the sand and the fiery sun had painted the sky with brush strokes of crimson orange before disappearing behind Table Mountain.

As we travelled the shimmering roads, I scoured the parched terrain for the twenty acres of land my father had bought to start a chicken farm soon after his arrival and wondered whether that was once his land. I always remember my mother explaining to me how a water diviner had visited the site to give his opinion on the presence of water and used a v-shaped stick to detect for it.

And I never thought it would happen but here I was visiting Kirstenbosch Gardens set against the awesomeness of the mountain, its grandeur making it one of my favourite haunts. We wandered the winding paths, took in the dazzling displays of plants and flowers indigenous to the Cape not to mention the pink tinged proteas with spiky velvet foliage that as a child I'd pick wild to take home to my mother. I also took delight loitering amongst the billowing silver trees that fringed the sweeping lawns where, after my christening on that sunny Sunday decades earlier, my parents had posed for photographs with me in their arms.

Travelling to Claremont to locate my first home was where my memories were strongest with every aspect unrecognisable from how I remembered it. I had a strong urge to ring the door-bell but the enormous signage warning intruders of security within deterred me. It resembled a fortress rather than a family home, my home. To connect with my childhood and the time when I had called my father 'Daddy' was what I longed for. And then I saw him whisk Connie off to a ball with my mother pleading to accompany him on her own and realized that still firmly lodged in my memory was that showdown.

From here we made our way to Newlands, the one mission high on my list to locate the state-of-the-art bungalow that my father had built when I was ten. My heart went into overdrive as we turned off Newlands Avenue and cruised into Pinewood Road. A cascading pale pink hibiscus tree was a new addition to the ex-terior but what astonished me was the high fencing that had sprung up around the perimeter; there were no protective measures when I lived there, just an open rustic fence. As chil-dren, we roamed freely with no thought to any danger, although I do recall my father kept a small black pistol in the top drawer of his bedside table. It saddened me to think the crime rate had esca-lated to such an extent that it called for such drastic measures and, as I investigated further, I realized it was not just my home that had succumbed to security. There was even an intercom at the main gates and as I pressed the buzzer and explained my rea-son for visiting I stood there open-mouthed with the discovery that the present owners, Rose and Martin Margolius, were the same couple my father had sold it to all those years ago. They welcomed us with open arms and as we gathered round the din-ing table for afternoon tea, I was awe-struck by the jagged mountainous backdrop with its haze of deepest green. It appeared much closer than I had remembered and awakened my apprecia-tion for the beauty of its setting.

In every room I entered, I could hear Connie's laughter, with that burst of freshness from her Ma Griffe perfume tingling my nostrils and then I smelt my mother's scrumptious home bak-ing that wafted down the corridor towards my bedroom, usually at weekends. And after my father put the bungalow on the market, I thought back to the current Jewish owners who, prior to moving in, had called round with a bag of bread and salt to put in the kitchen cupboard. They explained that the bread was a tradition so that the house would never know hunger and the salt was for life to always have flavour. It sounded fascinating but my father thought it absurd and wanted to throw it away but this time my mother won her case, telling him to leave it where it was.

I ventured into the back garden and noticed a swimming pool was now where my father's brick barbecue once stood and the lawn he'd taken so much pride in reminded me how the cicadas incensed him with their shrill, relentless whine on a hot summer's night. Grabbing the stainless-steel letter opener off our wrought iron hall table under cover of darkness he would get down on all fours and stab at the grass to silence them. Watching his antics was the one thing that always made my mother roar with laughter.

For the second leg of our holiday, we checked in to a chic apartment in fashionable Camps Bay. Three decades on, I realized how I'd taken this up market area for granted and how, on the nearby Robben Island, I had been oblivious to the indignation of Nelson Mandela's twenty-seven-year imprisonment who, as an anti-Apartheid activist, had fought for those who were disadvantaged by the system of racial segregation. Our visit coincided with his release a few months earlier and the subsequent dismantling of the regime, with Mandela leading his people to democracy amid renewed hope for a brighter future. At last, justice had prevailed.

We celebrated New Year in our apartment and with the end of the ruling came the first opportunity for people to rejoice, irrespective of colour. Rowdy revellers thronged the beaches below with loud chanting and exuberant celebrations continuing into the early hours of the morning. It was a wonderful spectacle to witness and although no-one slept much that night, we all shared in their joy.

While on this side of the peninsula, a trip to the summit of Table Mountain in the cable car was a priority. We'd had two abortive attempts because of its tablecloth of mist that descends without warning but finally, on a cloud free morning, the four of us made it to the top, all three and a half thousand feet of rocky escarpment that opened onto an unexpected plateau with lookout points over Cape Town's breath-taking modernity below. My diary entry read:

> 'Worth the wait even if it meant rising at 5.30 and queuing!'

My desire to re-establish a connection with my past had been like studying the splendour of my birthplace from the outside looking in. Through adult eyes, there was a magical beauty to the place I had never fully appreciated: I felt intoxicated with so many memories. I had tried for years to visualise what it would be like to revisit the land of my youth and I wasn't disappointed and to share my childhood with my family had been an exhilarating experience.

On 2 January 1995, my diary entry read:

> 'Our day to leave. A dream comes true.'

With the discovery of an upgrade to first class on our homeward flight, the children thought they were royalty, not to mention the caviar for lunch!

With tear-filled eyes, I bid farewell to my roots for a second time. And then I wrote:

> 'Approaching England invited into cockpit to talk with pilot. 7.30 am arrived Heathrow blanketed in frost.'

It wasn't long after arriving back in England that I had a phone call from Connie. 'How was the holiday? I couldn't stop thinking about you and all those times we shared together.'

For a moment I was unable to respond.

CHAPTER 18
LIFE IS UNFAIR

It seemed hard to believe when, five years later, in 1999, my mother and Howard put their Georgian semi on the market. It was a tough decision but the love nest that they referred to as paradise was proving too much upkeep. My children were saddened when they heard the news; it was a place they related to, not only from our time in Dorchester but they had fond memories splashing through the nearby shallow brook before visiting the farm to collect eggs with their granny and grandpa.

I recall the day well when I learnt that Howard was beginning to cause my mother concern. Chris and I had returned from helping at a charity plant sale at the home of Lesley Crowther, the television personality. Lesley was a great character with a booming voice, and it had become customary for him to offer his helpers a lift in his Rolls Royce. The time he picked us up was memorable; donning his straw boater, I imagined myself performing to an audience. He laughed in that cheerful fashion of his, clearly amused by my antics.

After returning home that evening the phone rang. It was my mother.

'I'm really worried.' She had not filled me in with any details beforehand, but she poured out her concerns. Not only had Howard shouted at her – and that I know would have frightened her – but he had also put the electric kettle on the electric hot plate.

Howard said he could not understand the necessity to relocate, but with early dementia diagnosed, the thought of moving swung from an excellent idea one day to the worst decision the following. My mother knew that being nearer family was crucial for their wellbeing and would simplify all our lives if we were not having to rush down at weekends.

The day they arrived at their warden controlled flat, built on the site that was once a lively cattle market in nearby Keynsham, I sensed my mother's eagerness to draw my attention to the new resting place of her 'personal box', reminding me she'd need to have a sort out when they were settled.

Just as Chris had done when I was twenty, Howard had given my mother a sense of purpose and was someone whom, over the years, I had grown fond of and had endless respect for. Not only was he my stepfather but he was a true gentleman who had given each one of us an acute awareness of just how precious our existence is on this earth. With an energetic enthusiasm, he gave of his time, not only to his own grandchildren, but also to our two who, through marriage, had become his extended family. I recall the time he helped my teenage son construct a fort in our garage as *Star Trekkin'* by the Firm played repeatedly. He thought he might go 'round the bend' but stuck it out and saw the model through to fruition. We had a good laugh about it only recently.

When Howard required permanent care, it broke my mother's heart to witness this one time highly skilled engineer in the Royal Navy now non-communicative and slumped in his chair, all of us agonising, knowing how he would have hated seeing himself in his present condition.

During the upheaval of moving, I received a phone call from my uncle Stan. By a strange coincidence, he informed me that my auntie Nancy was also in a nursing home. She too was suffering with dementia and since Stan was unwell himself, her needs had become a challenge. They were a wonderful couple, warm and loyal; Stan had looked like a dashing film star in his Merchant Navy uniform. The history we shared went back a long way, so I did not intend leaving it too long before seeing them. Still living in Mudeford, in a property that had once belonged to Stewart Granger, the film actor, it was always a pleasure to reminisce; that went for my mother and Howard, too, who they sometimes invited to holiday with them. They laughed from the time they arrived until the time they left; there was a joke about a four-legged chicken which I never did understand but my mother said their visits were a tonic.

Over coffee, Stan asked me to fetch his leather briefcase, which was propped against the Welsh dresser in the flag-stoned hallway. He had made an interesting discovery and presented the marriage certificate of my father's parents, Annie, and William Berry. The date was 1948 but they had tampered with it to make it appear they had married earlier. My father, their eldest, was born in 1918. With three children to their name we could not understand why they had only taken the decision to get married in 1948. It was inconceivable to think they had survived the gossip from the folk of Hereford during all those years. I thought back to Fanny's wish that my parents did not marry. Was she aware and was that the reason? We all agreed it was fascinating but that we would never know the truth.

When I offloaded my discovery to my mother, she appeared flabbergasted; she had never picked up on her in-laws' background. 'Wait till I tell Linda,' she laughed.

While my mother's health was failing, Connie's life was one continual adventure and after a voyage to Bermuda and Barbados, followed by a holiday to Cape Cod and the Algarve, she then wrote on her postcard from Cape Town:

> 'Disembarked QE2 yesterday after excellent trip. Sea calm, lovely cabin, pleasant company – too much food as usual. We called at St. Helena this time and had a lovely day. We all decided we would like to go again. We went out this morning to shop and lunch and going to Somerset West tomorrow to meet Maxine's mother-in-law. Love to all.'

(Maxine was the local tour guide who Connie had hired on previous visits to drive her to her favourite haunts.)

During the next five years, she enjoyed further cruises to Cape Town where Maxine invited her to stay with her family. Their friendship blossomed, and I was intrigued to read in one of Connie's letters that their three-year-old son had 'accepted me as part of the family.'

It dawned on me that I was the same age when Connie had

arrived in my home and then she went on:

> 'I am being urged on to stay, if not forever, at least for an-
> other month but I have resisted the temptation. I am due
> back at Manchester at the end of January. I just hope I
> don't have trouble with my overweight luggage. If the
> worse comes to the worst I may have to pay excess bag-
> gage, but I hope not.'

As with all Connie's acquaintances, they invited her into their
world.

By 2002, our relatives were fast approaching an impressive age
and it proved a troublesome year for my mother.

Having recovered from a hysterectomy she suffered another
set-back; with five adults monitoring her unsteady footsteps, she
fell in our lounge. It was Easter Sunday. With the discovery that
she had fractured her hip and wrist it became clear that rehabili-
tation would take time. 'Not sure what I've done to deserve this,'
she said.

During these demanding weeks, I was at home catching up
on the ironing one morning when a postcard dropped through the
letterbox. It was from Connie. The writing emblazoned on the
front read 'Greetings from sunny St. Lucia.' My stomach
churned.

> 'Cruising is the life. Having a wonderful time. Sea like a re-
> flective glass. Every bit as relaxing as voyage to Barbados.
> Terrifically hot yesterday but cooler today after tropical
> rainstorm. Being waited on hand and foot on banana Geest
> Line.'

I stamped on the postcard before hurling it across the room, asking myself why life could be so punishing to those who had always
put others first. It was obvious that over the years my mother's
health had taken a severe and irreparable battering from Connie's
continual involvement with my family; it was impossible to forgive
her knowing how my mother's emotional anxiety had impinged
on every aspect of my life too.

'I just can't think anymore,' my mother told me, 'I'm anxious all the time.' Martin, my mother's clinical psychologist, explained that her needs were becoming more complex and the evening she rang me to say she could not continue in the flat on her own, I rushed over to settle her and stay the night. In the morning, I telephoned Martin to explain she was at her wits' end. He suggested she would benefit from a spell of respite.

'I mean today, now,' he insisted. There was no option.

This magical place was in Bath. I was to take her immediately. It broke my heart but knew it was necessary before her health spiralled out of control again.

To witness Martin lifting my feeble mother into the passenger seat of my car was like a rapier going through me. She had always taken a pride in her appearance but her lank hair told me she no longer cared.

I sniffed back the tears as I drove her away from her flat. It was one of my toughest moments. What had I done? How could I be so heartless? A thousand thoughts flooded my head. I tried to reassure myself it was in her best interests but at the same time tussled with an overpowering guilt as I took her fragile arm and escorted her through the entrance doors into the care of someone she had never met.

Her one request was that I keep on eye on her box of correspondence … just while she was in there, she said.

With my mother's slow decline over the next few months it became clear that she would be unable to return to her apartment. She was like a bird with broken wings. Her once ice blue eyes which someone had stopped her on a bus to comment upon in her youth, had receded and dulled and her long, thick ebony hair I remember combing as a child was now a short, wispy pewter. But beneath this unkind appearance was a grace and poise with her gentle manner as caring as it had always been. Luckily, my mother still had her sense of humour and would sometimes have us all in hysterics, especially when she told us about one of the residents making off with her underwear and another who was convinced her spectacles were his spectacles, complaining he couldn't see a bloody thing.

With Connie still globe-trotting, in the chilly autumn of 2003 my mother was giving cause for concern. She had been vomiting;

whatever she ate disagreed with her. When the doctor called and explained she needed to go to hospital for observation, she pleaded with him to admit her the following morning, but he was adamant that she should go at once.

By three in the morning the medical staff advised that Chris and I leave. The doctor offered little information except to say they would do another assessment in the morning. Apart from telling us she felt light-headed, as though she was falling off the bed, my mother appeared alert. She too urged us to go home as we both had work the following day. 'You go darling. You'll be worn out.'

'Mum …' I tightened my grip on her bony shoulder.

'I'll be okay,' she reassured me. 'Just need a nap.'

Reluctantly we listened to her instructions with a hug and a promise that I would be back later that day.

The following morning, I was at my desk. It was 21 November 2003 and a Friday, the busiest day of the week in the school office. The early morning calls were coming in back to back with no time to ring the hospital. The phone rang again. I grabbed the receiver to offer my usual good morning greeting. It was not a parent; it was the hospital telling me to get there as soon as I could.

I don't recall the journey, but I was too late.

I requested to see my mother the minute I arrived. Cautiously, I parted the pale blue curtains drawn round her bed. I blinked back the tears and saw someone without a care in the world. I stood numbly at her bedside, absorbing the wonder of my incredible mother. I bent over to kiss her forehead and to thank her for everything she had sacrificed for my sake. Her face was serene, and she wore a half smile. Her hands still looked the same, velvety to the touch with protruding veins that as a child I would run my fingers across as though playing the harp. I might have missed holding her hand as she drew her last breath, but I took comfort knowing she was finally at peace with an expression of deep contentment that I would treasure for the rest of my days.

Half an hour later, with tears rolling down my flushed cheeks, I stumbled out of the hospital, alone and in shock, conscious only of my footsteps and sobs. I had her wedding ring zipped securely in my wallet and what belongings she had taken with her the previous evening still in her overnight holdall, untouched. I have tried to process that gruesome night. Listening to my mother's instructions. Walking away from someone who never walked away from me. Lying in that bed alone. Her leaving us without warning. The guilt. The unfairness.

Hearing that the diagnosis was carcinoma of the uterus I realized this must have been due to her refusal to have the radiotherapy after her hysterectomy; she said she didn't feel mentally strong enough to cope with the ordeal and told me she would 'take a chance'. Again, in my wisdom, I knew it was all to do with her broken nervous system from years ago.

In the week following my mother's death, I received a phone call. It was Connie. Every few weeks she would ask about the children so perhaps I had mentioned that my mother was not well. She was ringing to enquire. My grief was difficult to come to terms with and my feelings were still raw. It was a pain I had not experienced before and hearing her comforting words made me gasp. Tears dripped from the end of my nose and sharp sobs made talking impossible. I held the phone from my ear, trying to regain composure. I had neither the inclination nor the energy to discuss my mother. But Connie started singing her praises, telling me what a marvellous lady she was.

'We had some good times together,' she said. 'You didn't speak much of her to me, but she was often in my thoughts. She was a wonderful mother to you.'

Listening to her talk so well of my mother left me both moved and confused. And, yes, there was a mutual understanding between the pair of us that neither spoke about but that we both knew about; I made sure I never mentioned the past and it obviously hadn't gone unnoticed. I wondered if my mother's death had prompted her to say all this. Bearing in mind this was the person who had pushed my mother to breaking point, it's a pity she never thought to ask about her before. The way she was talking was strange; it all sounded so plausible, as though it had meant something to her. I am sure she did think about my mother and all the hurt she had inflicted although, at the time, it was a situation that had never appeared to bother her in the slightest. This was someone my mother must have wanted to throttle on so many occasions.

Connie's reaction defied belief.
Could it be her guilty conscience surfacing?

CHAPTER 19
STARTLING REVELATIONS

It was 20 February 2004. A message from my stepsister stopped me in my tracks. Howard had died. Again, it was a Friday the same day of the week my mother had died, only twelve weeks later.

I sat behind my desk digesting the news that this gentleman had abandoned his struggle with life. We had anticipated his death but with his healthy lifestyle he seemed reluctant to let go.

With my half term looming, news of Howard's passing had finally triggered my urge to sort through my mother's private correspondence, a job I had nagged myself to do for months. I would clear the unsightly boxes piled high in our spare room and in view of the fact my mother was a bit of a hoarder presumed much of it would be only worthy of the shredder. That was everything apart from her tatty Fairy Liquid box. I remember great significance she always placed on its whereabouts. Marked with a huge **PRIVATE** in thick felt tip on the lid she said it contained her personal papers.

When we packed up their Weymouth home, I can still visualise her saying, 'That box over there,' gesturing to the make-shift bookcase Howard had cobbled together from surplus shelving. 'It's coming with us in the car,' like it was a prized piece of sculpture. 'Not having it on the removal lorry.' Back in Weymouth, as I stood at her dining table wrapping her precious Coalport in bubble wrap, I remember the pair of us giggling when I asked her if it contained the crown jewels; I needed to inject a little light-heartedness into an awkward situation.

I tussled with my conscience and whether it was right to lay bare my mother's life, her past, her privacy, and her isolation on a continent from which there was no escape. I felt like a naughty schoolgirl about to venture into a prohibited area for which I should obtain her permission, knowing that once in the open there would be nothing confidential about it any longer. But I consoled myself with the fact my mother did not have any secrets. Yes, my parents had a troubled marriage, which I had witnessed first-hand, and then there was their fiery divorce which followed years later but I knew all that.

So, with scissors poised in one hand and a strong black coffee in the other, I sat on the bedroom floor studying the box as though it was a holy shrine. What intrigued me was why she had written 'private'. I guessed there might be treasured letters like we all have, sometimes too difficult to discard. As I cut the thick string, the flaps sprang open to reveal a white postcard on the top. It had my name written across it. The sight of my mother's writing made my hand recoil. It was in heavy black ink as though she did not want me to miss it. 'DIANE. FOR YOUR BOOK ONE DAY?'

I held my breath. Was she up there having a laugh!

The last time I'd found an envelope in her handwriting was the one she'd left on my pillow when I was living in Sea Mills; that earth-shattering afternoon after I'd returned from work and discovered she had vanished. There was nothing wrong with her memory right up to her last day, so I prayed more than anything that this was her way of having fun and letting me know she'd remembered my childhood threats that one day I would put everything down in print.

Seeing my name printed in her wobbly hand brought a lump to my throat. I wondered when she had written it and, what was even more significant, why she had written it.

Worn string secured neat bundles of correspondence; two hefty piles had frayed yellowing ribbon tied round them while perished rubber bands bunched others together. There was even a collection of letters I had written and as I rummaged, I spotted my mother's diaries written in her neat hand. I also recognised her beloved Howard's handwriting. It was small and neat in his bright blue Quink ink. I whipped one of his letters from the top of the pile, all of them tied neatly with a red bow. I prized it uneasily from its envelope. 'To my beloved Sweetheart Bee...' it said but because Howard had just died it did not seem right to investigate further.

When I saw the stack of official business letters from a solicitors' firm marked on the outside of the envelope 'private and confidential', my heart skipped a beat. My mother had never talked about any aspect of her divorce and, although I was aware that it had become a thorny issue, back in the seventies there was never any mention of it.

I extracted the pristine document from its buff envelope.

A letter confirmed the enclosure of her Decree Absolute dated 31 January 1974, attached to which my mother had pinned foolscap sheets detailing events in support of her divorce. I read on.

And then I caught the word ADULTERY.

I broke out in a cold sweat.

My eyes flew back to the top of the page to check the name. Berry v Berry.

On the grounds of Adultery. That was what it said.

Clutching the document, I glanced round the room to check it was not a weird dream.

The words screamed at me as I reread them for the umpteenth time:

> 'Mr and Mrs Berry were married in March 1940, there being one child of the family who is now over 21. Mrs Berry left her husband in June 1970, and I am asked to advise on the prospects of her obtaining a divorce on the ground of his conduct during the marriage.
>
> It seems that during the war, when Mr Berry was serving in the R.A.M.C., he met a Miss Bassett and became friendly with her. I have the impression that Mrs Berry knew Miss Bassett and was aware that her husband was friendly with her but had no reason to suppose that there was anything sinister in the association.
>
> In 1948 the Berry's emigrated to South Africa. In 1952

Miss Connie Bassett went out to stay with them. Mrs Berry objected violently to this but was told it was only for a holiday. In fact, Miss Bassett took a job out there and continued to stay with the Berry's more or less continuously until 1963. It seems that throughout this period Mr Berry committed adultery with Miss Bassett regularly, admitting as much to his wife. Mrs Berry objected frequently to the situation but was told by her husband that it was none of her business and that he wanted Miss Bassett out there whether his wife liked it or not.'

A disbelieving truth began to emerge. I swallowed hard as nausea rose in my gullet.

'It also appears that apart from the liaison with Miss Bassett, Mr Berry was during this period treating his wife with active cruelty. It seems there were frequent outbursts of bad temper and on about four occasions there was actual physical violence. At all events Mrs Berry was greatly upset by her husband's behaviour to the extent she suffered nervous breakdowns on two occasions. She put up with the situation, however, because she was entirely dependent on her husband and more importantly for the sake of her daughter.'

Cruelty? When the hell had that happened? I knew my father had a violent temper, as he proved when he collected ants with his brother Billy as a youngster and had cracked him over the head with a shovel because he had more than his fair share. But as for cruelty in the home, I had never witnessed anything. I mined my memory for clues that I might have overlooked along the way but the only incident I could recall was when Grandma was staying with us in Surrey and in one of his rages, he threatened to kill my mother.

'In 1963 the Berry's returned to England and it seems that Miss Bassett also returned with them. For the next two and a half years the Berry's lived in Birmingham and Surrey. Miss Bassett evidently had a flat in London during this pe-

riod, visiting the Berry's fairly often and from time to time
Mr Berry would spend the night with Miss Bassett at her
flat.

In 1966 when the Berry's moved to the Bristol area Mr
Berry had arranged for Miss Bassett to join the household
once more. Mrs Berry was not aware of this until the move
took place. She continued to endure the situation, humiliat-
ing though it was because she was anxious to see her
daughter grown up before the marriage broke down. In
1968 she hinted to her daughter that she might leave, but
the latter 'implored her to stay' for the time being. If I understand the position correctly at about this time Mrs Berry
found herself a job in Bath and also accommodation but
Mr Berry found out about this and promised that things
would improve.

Shortly after this the household moved to Sea Mills where
Mr Berry acquired a shop cum post office, Mrs Berry the
wages clerk and Miss Bassett the post mistress. Mrs Berry
was becoming increasingly conscious of the indignity of her
situation, informing her husband in a letter she wrote to
him that his attitude towards her was one of indifference.

Matters came to head in January 1970. Mrs Berry's aunt
had died, and she had attended the funeral despite being
told by her husband that if she did, she would be finished
in the business. A few days later there was a terrible row in
which Mr Berry told her to leave and take a furnished flat
elsewhere.'

It was a shocking show down. I had rushed to shut the windows so
the neighbours could not hear his tirade. Knowing my mother
had endured the crippling situation until I was twenty-one deserved a medal.

'It is important that some corroboration be obtained. By
far the most obvious source is the daughter. She is in a better position than anyone to assess the situation prevailing in
the household and evidence from her would carry great
weight. It is possible that she will feel reluctant to give evidence against her father. On the other hand, I am told that

sympathies were with her mother. At all events she would certainly be worth approaching.'

My blood curdled to think the solicitor suggested he consult with me. Again, my mother must have refused, just another example of her protecting me and keeping all details of the past hidden.

My father was a heartless man to try to prevent my mother from attending her aunt's funeral. It was inconceivable to think he could act in that way. There were instances I could relate to, awkward moments I could remember and troubled scenes I had witnessed but never had I observed brutality towards my mother.

Not only that but the official correspondence compiled by my mother's solicitor documented that my father had:

> 'Permitted the said Connie Bassett to remain in the household although he well knew that his wife was greatly distressed and humiliated thereby. On a number of occasions, he told her that nothing and no-one would part him from 'Connie', no matter what the outcome might be. From 1952 [that's when Connie had arrived in Cape Town] he had treated his wife with increasing indifference and lack of affection, making it plain that in his eyes she took second place to the said Connie Bassett.'

I then digested a letter from my father's solicitor which documented:

> 'his client alleges that it is Mrs Berry who had committed a matrimonial offence.'

My father had obviously got wind that Howard was on the scene. How I have no idea as I made sure never to utter a word and thankfully, he never enquired. After all his wrongdoing over the years, it was preposterous to think he was accusing my mother of being the guilty party. From the gist of legal correspondence, it seemed he was not prepared to let my mother go without a fight. A further letter I came across in draft form was to my mother's solicitor informing him of her meeting with my father in the park.

'How I felt sick at the thought of coming face to face with him as I had no idea what his mood might be and what might develop. Surprisingly, he apologised for his behaviour of the past few months. I can never remember him doing such a thing before. He was all for me packing up and returning home with him immediately. However, although his apologies and promises sounded reasonable he said nothing about the future, and I sensed that within a short while the old routine would quickly develop with me taking second place to Connie. I said I had no intention of returning home with him. The meeting ended but as I made to leave the car his attitude changed. He said he would be suing me for divorce based on my desertion.'

And then I unearthed proof of the cruelty my father had inflicted, namely when I was four. It seemed that when I was attending kindergarten my mother had not sent me on one occasion as it was pouring with rain. My father demanded an explanation and then proceeded to 'land severe blows across her face.' He had, on another occasion, thrown her out of the bedroom – he was making some protest about the street lamp outside although it was difficult to understand what that had to do with my mother – and a public rebuke years later when she worked in the shop and he saw her eating a boiled sweet. This instance demonstrated to my mother that although he had obtained his ambition (business and Miss Bassett) he still regarded her as a source of his discontent. She pointed out how she had to manage on insufficient housekeeping and no personal allowance and how he had not spoken to her for days, once for twelve weeks, taking his meals separately. It was also itemised how 'Miss B' followed us everywhere, holidays, cinema, theatre, dinners, outings and, after her arrival, there had been no terms of endearment or loving gestures.' My mother summed all this up with the word 'Breakdown.'

Like wreckage strewn across a cruel sea I studied the evidence before me.

I was determined that Connie was not going to get away with her crime. She would be offering me an apology for the suffering she had caused not only to me, but also to my mother, someone who would never hurt a fly. Surely, she would want to undo her past mistakes. It was the least she could do, and I hoped she would have the courage and the decency to seek mercy for the lives she had destroyed.

Reeling from my outrageous discovery, I knew that whatever father/daughter relationship there had been back in the times when he called me his angel had now withered. To think my father had caused my mother such appalling cruelty was grotesque, and the fact Connie was involved without any qualms was even more disturbing.

I rushed to make another cup of coffee and then sat down to reread the words hoping somehow, they had changed their meaning.

Divorce granted on the grounds of adultery ... for *twenty something years*. You mean to say my father had been carrying on with this woman, my auntie Connie whom I had grown up with and, what is more, the person I had trusted and loved. And who, it would appear, had not the slightest intention of leaving once she set foot in our home.

It infuriated me to think my mother had not breathed a word about the past. I thought I knew her and everything there was to know about her. We'd always been open with one another, or so I presumed, so it was impossible to understand why she had always kept me in the dark but concluded it was because she was a private lady and, like me now, too ashamed to disclose the truth about Connie's adulterous relationship with my father. Another possibility, I guess, was the emotional impact it might have had on me as a child. I racked my brain to see whether she had ever hinted about the real reason for this intruder's presence but the closest she ever got to dribbling the truth was when she'd sit me down for a chat and try to make me see that her life was not a normal existence. Her words were always the same. Although economical with the truth, I sensed she hoped I might bite so she could elaborate. Crushed by an overwhelming sense of guilt, I sat and pondered why I never probed further when all I could ever do was nod in agreement, terrified that if we got into a full-blown discussion, she would tell me she was leaving.

I was struggling with the psychological bullying and claustrophobic existence my mother had lived through. Rarely had I seen her feelings surface. I can only assume she managed to survive by pretending the situation did not exist.

I flung open the back door and inhaled the blustery air to control my anger. Horrendous as it was, somehow it wouldn't have been so torturous for my mother had my father conducted his heinous affair away from our home but the fact he was rubbing her nose in it under the same roof made it even more abhorrent and to tell her it was none of her business was beyond monstrous.

I began to understand the scenario through adult eyes and the real reason for the many arguments, not because my parents had become incompatible, but arguments that carried a much greater significance; my mother's understandable hostility for this brazen woman walking into her marriage and my father's inexcusable attitude towards her, a person who, timid at the best of times, was no match for his brick-wall arrogance. I wanted my mother back so that, now I knew everything, we could talk openly.

I had grown up in a home that carried an ugly label: a ménage a trois. The bitterness I felt towards a father who had betrayed his only daughter was indescribable. I wanted to scream and let everyone know what a beast he had been.

Looking back, it was little wonder my mother had been eager for me to know the whereabouts of her personal box.

So, Connie was his mistress. I found myself confirming out loud what I had just read. It made me shudder to think my father had been at it during all those years. A growing sense of disgust came over me as I visualised the pair of them together, wondering where and how they had achieved their shameless affair; was it to some secluded cove after my father collected her from work, where they would make love and then return home without a shred of guilt or was it kept for night time when he crept furtively along the corridor to her bed, me fast asleep in the adjoining room, with the thrill of the liaison fuelling their passion?

I would never be able to tell Chris about my weird background. The hurt and upset was not something I wanted to share with my husband. Although guilt-ridden, he might insist that I tell the children and that was out of the question.

Now I could understand why my father had lost the friendship of countless acquaintances during those early times in Cape

Town and the friends who didn't walk away were no doubt the type who saw no wrong. It was little wonder he had also lost the respect of his own brother and sister and their respective other halves but for him the sacrifice meaningless compared to his relationship with Connie. He had what he wanted, his wife and a mistress.

It made me question the dynamics of their affair, who drove who and what this woman had that my mother did not, but perhaps my mother had it all and my father simply craved a double dose.

I dug deeper into the musty box and unearthed a wad of letters scribbled in pencil in draft form on lined foolscap paper, two of which were of significance. The first was in Howard's writing for my mother to send to Chris. It brought everything home to me when I read it:

> 'Perhaps by now you will have learnt from Diane of her fear that I have decided to take the necessary action that I spoke to you about previously, namely, to seek a home of my own.
> Would you please afford her the comfort she most desperately needs at this stage? Perhaps even to explain why I have acted so and the reasons why I cannot delay much longer this regretful but necessary step.
> I shall always be eternally grateful.
> Yours truly,'

The second letter, again in draft form, my mother had addressed to me. I must have received the original, but I cannot recall it. She explained about her future with Howard and how it would not affect our special mother/daughter relationship, if that were my concern, and how she loved me and always would. And how nothing, but nothing, would ever come between us.

I felt ashamed and racked with guilt when I thought back to my initial resentment of Howard. I made no secret of my feelings when I discovered he was on the scene but, being an impressionable teenager, I was thinking only of myself. Had I known the reason for my mother's misery during the countless years of growing up, I might have viewed their liaison from a different perspective and been delighted that she had found such a rare gem.

I had still not dared to open the letters Howard had written to his beloved Blanche; one it would appear for every day of the week they were apart. I felt I could not cope with that so decided to leave it until another time.

But at a quick glance, his letters looked intriguing.

Diane Harding

CHAPTER 20
REFLECTING

How did I feel after reading the solicitor's correspondence? Like a mad dog wanting to tear my father apart. And as for Connie? I fled upstairs and took great satisfaction cutting into smithereens the leopard print scarf she had given me during her time in Southport. I did not want her gifts. What I wanted was for her to show remorse for her part in the sordid affair.

Strong memories of those early times in Cape Town flooded my mind. I tried hard to focus on the happy times when my parents looked lovingly down on me at my christening, doted on me as a baby, bathed me, and strolled with the pram through shady parks. And on occasions when I couldn't get to sleep at night, how my father would rock me in his arms and with his soothing tone sing me a lullaby to thank me for being an angel.

To get things in perspective, I felt compelled to reread the letters Linda had unearthed. Everything began to make sense, including the reasoning behind my mother's visits to the farm at Franschhoek and with her battered nervous system why she'd become blighted by superstition, tapping her dressing table several times for good luck before leaving the room.

The extent of my innocence was ridiculous. I was embarrassed for my dysfunctional family and for the shame my home carried. I felt naïve, gullible, stupid, and furious knowing I had been so blinkered. And because my father always referred to

Connie as Con Con and she called me Di Di it did not strike me as unusual. The more I thought about it the more things began to slot into place. That must have been the reason why, when we went camping, my father always insisted he take Connie with him to collect the wood for the campfires. I could never understand why my mother paced up and down outside the tent waiting for them to return and why it took so long with only a handful of sticks to show for their labours. And when we went on our excursions to Gordon's Bay, could that have been why my father always refused to allow me to accompany him to choose my ice cream from the nearby café but instead preferred to run off with Connie? I could never work out why buying them took so long. I then began to think back to my time in Birmingham and Surrey when my father often returned home late from work and my mother would roll her eyes and tell me that it was another meeting.

I began to question why it was I had never heard footsteps creeping along corridors or doors closing quietly in the dead of night. Whenever we had violent thunderstorms when I was a little girl, perhaps that was the reason it was always my mother who scooped me up and carried me into her bed in case I should notice my father was not asleep in his.

It was late afternoon. I knew I would have to pretend as though it had been a normal day.

I had unconsciously shoved the evidence back into its box. I could not face anything else for the time being. Had I not pried into my mother's private box I would be none the wiser. But I had laid bare the facts, and these were the consequences I would have to live with.

'Get a grip Diane!' I screamed. I was still in shock but needed to snap out of it. Chris would be home from work any minute. Two streaked cheeks glared back at me in the mirror. I looked washed out. I rushed to my bedroom to put the brush through my hair and pop on a bit of lipstick. I needed to behave as though nothing out of the ordinary had happened.

My pressing urge to tell someone, anyone, was still with me but how could I open up to the world and reveal to everyone that 'Yes, Connie was my father's mistress,' and 'Yes, she lived with us during the affair,' and 'Yes, they'd been at it for over two decades.' That someone could only be Chris and I knew that by the time he arrived home I would be unable to find the courage.

What I longed for more than anything was to pick up the phone and discuss my revelation with a sibling.

'Quel jour!' I announced the second Chris breezed in the front door.

'What's …'

'Just open that bloody bottle of Sauvignon,' I said. 'And make it a large.

I spent the next few days reflecting on my findings. It was hard to put into words how I felt and although torturous to revisit the solicitor's correspondence, I needed to crack on with my investigation before I was back at school. What caught my eye in the bottom of the box was a bundle of letters I had written to my mother after she left Sea Mills, addressed to her sister's home near Leatherhead in Surrey, the place she'd escaped to on that horrifying day in question. The first one read:

> 'Dear Mum
> I am in an absolute shattered state for I am sure you have gone to Freda's for longer than a week … and when I hinted to Connie you had left, she simply wouldn't believe me and said you'd never do such a thing. When I woke up this morning, I had a cry to think you weren't here. I'm missing you desperately.'

I then went on to say:

> 'I can hardly think what to say and can only hope that it is not true. I had to tell Miss Butterfield, of course, because I was in such a state this morning. She said that perhaps it's the change of life making you do this. I just can't imagine what my life will be without you. Please once again, as I write this sobbing and with tears in my eyes, don't leave. I send you all my love and remember that I'm missing you terribly.'

I had forgotten the begging letters but not the trauma. It seemed unimaginable to think I had lived through all this. In the next one I had written:

> 'Dear Mum
> Thanks for your shattering letter I received this morning and proceeded to read, horror struck, sitting on the bottom stair.'
> [She must have sent me another letter in the post apart from the one I found on my pillow.] 'I am so sorry that everything has had to turn out this way for you Mum dear and can only say that I really do admire you for what you've done, but so desperately sorry on the other hand. I didn't realize that everything had got on top of you to quite such an extent. Please keep cheerful with the strain of things. (I can't help thinking that the bad weather has got you down too.)'

And then I let it all pour out:

> 'I have had a most worrying time, not eating and just star-ing into space for inspiration. Friday morning, I simply couldn't stand the thought of breakfast so staggered to work on an empty stomach in a dazed and shocked state, with my eyes feeling like two hard boiled eggs. I was so up-set during the morning that I was unable to invigilate at a B. Ed exam. (Actually, I wasn't going to work on Friday but did so because we had so much urgent work.) Miss But-terfield was very sympathetic and took me out to lunch because I didn't want to have lunch at the College. I can't tell you how much I am missing your lovely face round the house. You know how attached I am and how much I love you so please reconsider what you have done. I was staring into the buses that came past on Saturday while I was do-ing the shopping, in the hope that I might see you standing there ready to get off. All I could do was hope.'

I must have been frantic to write so many persuasive letters. Over the years, I have tried to put those memories to the back of my mind, sometimes successfully but often coming back to trouble me.

I had been biding my time before speaking to Linda, but it was now my turn to tell her of my findings. 'I've just spent my half term investigating Mum's private box. I've unearthed disturbing information,' I explained. 'I'd no idea my father was such a monster. I need to hear your take on events as it's crucial evidence for my writing!'

The other end of the phone went quiet as though her memory cogs were firing.

And then I found myself asking whether it was right to expose people's past in this way. It had become a moral dilemma but I consoled myself that it would be my way of informing those who had known my family from way back just what it was that must have become the subject of so much intrigue over so many years. At last I would be able to explain how this so-called visitor of ours had slotted into the puzzle and the real reason she had become suctioned to my family like a limpet to a rock. Perhaps it was Connie's goal all along to marry my father and the reason she had never relinquished her hold on him knowing that one day, whenever that was, she would become Mrs Berry and that her pleading for my mother's return after she left home was merely a decoy.

'Look, if I pop up and collect you at the weekend, hopefully we can discuss everything then.'

A fidgety night allowed me to rise early. It was a pleasant sunny drive through the scenic Slad Valley, home and final resting place of the author Laurie Lee, and before I knew it, Linda was out to greet me with her usual enthusiasm and tightly curled hair neatly in place. With no family of her own, she was a strong and confident lady, full of energy despite being in her early eighties.

She put a hand on my shoulder and ushered me inside, the dark bags under my eyes a giveaway.

'I can't help thinking about all those wasted years for poor Mum,' I said plonking myself down on the arm on her settee.

'D'you know, since your call, I've been racking my brains to see just how far back I *can* remember. I've had sleepless nights myself churning things over after all these years. And those letters I gave you ... your poor mother always sounded so desperate. I could never make your father out; he didn't seem to care what he was doing, just so long as he got his way. I still think about it even now.'

The heartache for my mother returned as I listened to Linda reflecting on those intolerable times and how helpless she and her mother had felt. She explained my mother's frustration when she prayed that Connie would see reason to return to England.

We talked non-stop during our journey to Bath and after a hasty lunch I frog-marched Linda to the rustic seating area at the bottom of the garden amidst the gentle hum of bees and a powerful scent of honeysuckle. In sunglasses and a floppy brimmed hat, I studied my aunt expectantly.

'Ready?' I asked with my spiral notebook and Bic pen poised for action.

'Well, I'll do my best,' she chuckled. 'Mind you. It's over sixty years. And you must remember my age, Diane. Don't forget I've had my own life to live.'

'It's hard to believe someone could arrive for a holiday and never leave.' I found myself repeating what I already knew.

And then Linda recounted the tale from when her mother was holidaying with us in Cape Town. 'You'd all gone to the beach and your father was feeding Connie grapes, like some Greek Goddess, and as a joke he popped a pebble in her mouth and then the pair of them fell about laughing. That's when Mother couldn't contain her anger and had a word with him.'

'Well I've got something to tell you.'

Linda turned to face me.

'Chris and I decided to investigate the *Union Castle*'s arrivals and departures and discovered that after Connie first set foot in Cape Town in March 1952 she came back to England and left Southampton to return again in July 1952; it was on her birthday, four months after her initial arrival in Cape Town. I presume she returned to England to collect her belongings.'

'She did! She came back to do just that. Poor Blanche must have despaired.'

I reflected on those fond farewells when as a two-year-old my father had waved me and my mother off on our momentous trip to England, knowing that would be the last time we would be a family of three.

As I tried to untangle my raging emotions, Linda admitted that she had been planning to talk to me. 'But I'm afraid I've been putting it off. Every time I come and stay, I think it'll be my opportunity. You know, sit down, just the two of us, but the timing has never been quite right.'

Knowing I had read the solicitor's correspondence, Linda appeared happy to discuss decades old events.

'Do you think my father thought he could get away with his shenanigans?'

'Honestly? I do. Blanche prayed Victor would realize what a fool he'd been. But she was no match for him, so I believe she felt it was easier to turn a blind eye and accept the situation. Not through choice mind you. I know I couldn't do it, but of course she had nowhere to go. *You* know how awkward your father could be. He was a dictatorial man. It must have driven poor Blanche crazy so when she came to England, when you were about eleven, Mother tried to persuade her to stay but of course, without you, it was out of the question.'

That would have been when we lived in Newlands. The thought of her going away was more than I could bear; I remember crying into my pillow at night to stifle the sound.

'She couldn't wait to get back to you, regardless of what was in store for her. Said she'd just have to face the music, but it took some pluck.' Hearing about her monumental sacrifice tugged at my heart.

Linda went on to explain that when my mother first emigrated 6,000 miles away, she thought it would be far enough to forget about Connie and too far for her to get in the way of her marriage. And another snippet she told me was how, during our time in England, a neighbour had spotted my father and Connie walking hand in hand along the road. That was the moment I knew they were both as fearless as one another; their gutsiness defied belief.

Linda discussed Connie at length. 'The woman didn't have a sprig of moral fibre. She was a typical femme fatale with no misgivings about crashing into someone else's marriage. Blanche always prayed she'd meet someone and bugger off. And have you told the children about any of this?' Linda was intrigued to know their reaction.

'Blimey, I've not let Chris in on it yet.'

I started to explain about the Literacy Course I'd recently attended in Bath Library and when asked to compile a short story I'd chosen a condensed version of my past, not realizing that I would have to share it with everyone round the table.

'It was a eureka moment. I could not believe I'd given away a slice of my life.'

After that, my conscience gnawed at me. I wanted my secret to remain stashed in my private little world, but I had begun to realize that the longer the silence, the harder it would be to unshackle myself.

I considered why it was so hard to let go. And then it hit me. My mother had been secretive with me and now I was doing the same to Chris. I told myself it was human nature to keep secrets. Besides, I needed to consider his reaction when I told him. What would he think of me, least of all my family? I was also concerned in case my flawless marriage suffered. We never settled our differences of opinion with an argument, so I didn't want to cause friction because I'd been withholding my past for so long. There was also the possibility that disclosing my grubby secret would be more painful than keeping it hidden; it would mean revisiting my childhood and delving into every background detail which was not a topic I felt at ease with. And because I had developed a coping mechanism by pretending it never happened, I knew that speaking about it would make it real. But I had read that harbouring secrets could be bad for your health and sleep patterns which could lead to emotional mood swings. The prognosis did not sound good. It was time to offload.

After my chat with Linda I got up to stretch my legs, but she remained seated.

'There *is* something else I think I ought to tell you.'

I wiped the globules of perspiration from my brow. I had no idea what to expect.

'Well,' she said. 'I'm going back to when you were born. We'd waited anxiously for news of your arrival and I remember shortly after your birth Blanche writing home – there was no phoning people back in those days – to tell us the good news and that your father was over the moon. She said he was acting like a little boy *and* so relieved you were a girl. Apple of his eye you were. And, for whatever reason, he did not want a boy. We were never quite sure why. Well ...' Linda appeared reluctant to spit it out. 'I've thought long and hard about telling you, but I think ...' Linda stopped mid-sentence. 'I think it's important I do.'

'Go on.' I braced myself.

'Well, as time went on ...,' her voice faltered as she tried to regain composure, 'and Connie became a household name, your father informed your mother you ... you were to remain an only child. Blanche said it came out of the blue.'

'What d'you mean?'

'He refused to let your mother have any more children!'

I shot to my feet. 'Wouldn't let her have ...?'

'No!'

'Why?'

'He said it wouldn't be fair on Connie!'

'Fair on Connie! What the *hell* had it got to do with her?' I turned away and snatched at a dandelion. A horrendous thought flashed through my mind. Had she ever fallen ...? No. I had to wipe such a heinous notion from my thinking. But trying to erase such thoughts was easier said than done. I could not let the matter drop and considered whether Connie had ever succumbed to an abortion, perhaps more than one back in those days. Was that the reason for her extended absence to the Lebanon where Judy told me she became a lady's companion? Worse still, was the unsettling possibility that I may have half-siblings somewhere out there who had perhaps been given up for adoption all those years ago.

Or was it me over-reacting?

'I'd always wondered why I was an only child.'

'Can you believe he'd insist on such a thing? So brutal, especially as Blanche told me how she'd have loved you to have a brother or sister. He must have been as hard as nails, but then, so was she. They say it takes one to know one. I'm sorry landing you with this but felt it important you knew all the facts but I never for one moment thought it would fall on me to tell you.'

Molten fury burned inside me as I took on board my father's stingy demand. The misery my lovely mother must have gone through gouged at my heart. Making a conscious decision not to have any more children was one thing; to deprive her of her motherly right was something quite different. It was impossible to fathom out my father's reasoning. Did he envisage jealousy between the two women or was it Connie's idea?

I couldn't help thinking it was lucky I came along when I did, otherwise my mother would have been childless. It was outrageous to think the pair of them had been accountable for my solitary days and the countless times I'd longed for a sibling; especially during my mother's ailing health, someone to share the responsibilities and to discuss the inevitable decisions that had to be made along the way and, right now, so we could squirm together.

I began to understand that there is a reason behind everything and how as an only child growing up in those difficult circumstances my self-esteem had been affected. And because of my father's selfish behaviour I'm convinced that must have been the reason for my shy nature; making new friendships with every new school was a challenge. I was cautious in the extreme and sometimes more fragile than those with boisterous siblings. With my temperamental nature, I would often burst into tears which is why my father nicknamed me Sarah Bernhardt after the French actress. I hate flying. I hate lifts. I assume that was something my mother had instilled in me with her nervous nature.

My mind darted back to the photograph albums I had flicked through on countless occasions. Was that the reason there were no photographs of us as a family after Connie's arrival in Cape Town? Was that something else my father considered unfair? There were photographs of me with my mother and Connie but none that featured me with just my parents and only one I could find of me with my father. I felt sad for other families who may be in that same position with nothing to look back on. Ripping out Connie's photos and tearing them to shreds gave me immense satisfaction.

Diane with her father in the park, Claremont, 1963

I wandered back up the garden in a daze. I needed to regain my composure and clear my head so excused myself for half an hour. I donned my new running shoes, slammed the front door, and jogged to the top of our road. Picking my way through the overgrown snicket and down the forty-nine steep concrete steps – I counted every one of them – I reached the calming ambience of the Avon. With the view of Kelston Hill to my left and a terrace of handsome Victorian properties to my right, the rhythmic patter of my stride and two sleek rowing boats whooshing towards the lock gates dominated the silence. Dodging the snoozing mallards along the cropped grassy bank by the ancient Brass Mill, once famous for the transportation of iron, I decided it would be bangers and mash for tea.

I remember once reading that throughout your life, you don't remember the days, but you certainly remember the moments. I could relate to that.

After driving Linda back to Cheltenham, I pondered on the bundle of Howard's letters, yet untouched and if I thought analysing the correspondence was going to be straightforward, I could not have been more wrong.

Diane Harding

CHAPTER 21
LOVE LETTERS

I t astounded me to discover that the first of Howard's letters I extracted from a collection dated 1968 had been sent to my mother while we were living in Saltford, but addressed to a post office box number in Bath, no doubt to keep their liaison a secret. And there were dozens more all of them revealing his extraordinary depth of passion.

Howard had a gift for words.

'My Darling
Once in a while two people meet and from a chance remark or glance – or lift of the head – there develops a fascination for each other's company. Such my dearest was our meeting. I remember it well.

There is nothing uncommon in this, except that it happened to us and that makes it more than wonderful: for each wooded lane and patterned field reminds one of the many times since, when we found in each other's company the need for each other.

The longing to be with you is no less now than when I first met you. It dominates my thinking and I unashamedly admit that you are on my mind constantly. Small wonder then is that when you phone me my heart skips a beat and I imagine you beside me. The hundred things I want to say escape me and all too soon the illusion breaks down.

But what is to become from our chance meeting? At first, I believed the signs pointed to S.A. [South Africa], and may still do so, although the initial overtures are not convincing. There are however a hundred other ways each presenting a possible road. The problem is which is the right one? Will chance that brought us together complete the manoeuvre or do we have to pull our own strings? Je ne sais quoi.
One thing is certain, that is, life without you is no life at all. I love you so very much.
Forever xxxx'

And then I discovered a letter that thoroughly unsettled me. Undated, Howard had written:

'My thoughts were of you and of your account of the tirade raged against you on your return home. Two people against one you said: verily you have a proverbial 'cuckoo in the nest'. I tried to reason out why it was that V should pursue a deliberate policy – as a despot – to superimpose a slave labour routine. Even he must see that this is a hell-bent collision course that must be heard out at some time.'

This must have been before my mother made her escape from Sea Mills when my father had lambasted her with another outburst, not only my father but also Connie. This alarmed me as I had never come across her siding with my father, certainly not in front of me.
His letter continued:

'Each day I say to myself the hours will soon pass – and the days too – when then I can enjoy you once again. To feel your arms, your lips, your hands – all of you around me, about me, to whisper in your ear every word passed between us these last tumultuous weeks……..What gluttons we are for punishment – what joy however can there possibly be with out each other……To these magic moments I am indebted for evermore because simple as they may seem they have over the past year permitted a greater awareness of each other's needs and of our understanding.'

I found myself engrossed in Howard's longing to be with his sweetheart ... forever.

> 'Quite naturally darling I am impatient to be with you again. A human weakness I know, but forgivable for to know you is to experience joy supreme....... It looks as though our dream of being together is beginning to be possible...One thing is certain that is we both need each other and will continue to do so irrespective of what the future brings......It cannot be wrong to take you away from your present burden to a more pleasant and amiable existence. It cannot come too soon for I am loathed to be parted from you a second more than I have to. With you I am 'King for the day'.
> God bless. All my love xxx'

Whilst Howard's letters spelt out his deep love for my mother, others charted his emotion for my mother's imprisonment and, from what I could make out, feelings he had penned for her every day of the week, sometimes more when they were apart. And once we had moved to Sea Mills, again he sent his correspondence to a post office box number, this time in Bristol. He even suggested times when it would be safe to ring one another from call boxes, or, even more daring, from their respective homes.

> 'Try ringing me at home Tuesday morn between 9.15 and 9.30. [That would be at his home as, at that point, he had not left his wife] Make it sound as if it is a call from my office or an office near by and you wish to speak to me. This is exceedingly difficult darling, but I expect it will be the pattern of events over the ensuing months before we get some satisfaction.'

From the gist of Howard's letters, it became clear that he appeared willing for my mother to take her turn in looking after her own mother, Fanny, to relieve Freda and Linda of their duties. He finished by saying:

'I can take Mother and would be delighted to do so. There are of course a number of other points on your side of the house that need careful thought. We both need courage and terrific patience. Please give my kindest regards to Mother. I hope she is well, and I wish her contentment. If she has you to look after her then she is doubly blessed.'

That was another twist I had not known about. And then:

'It would seem that I must love you very much indeed for how else can I explain why I should leave my golf bag at the club house instead of taking it to the car or for what other reason would there be for me to put on odd socks after changing. In truth I long for the sound of your voice and the warmth of having you near me. It seems that tomorrow, Tuesday, will never come. Perhaps you can meet me at Temple Meads for a quiet chat. Should there be any change of plan then I will get in touch with you on Thursday morning 9 – 9.15. I am really longing to be with you. To hold you, mmm. Such pleasures are worth a King's ransom. Cheerio my darling. God Bless and keep wishing.'

Not only that, but there was also mention of hiring beach huts at Bournemouth and Burton Bradstock. Goodness me. I could not believe it was my mother I was reading about.

'We have yet to obtain a beach hut … but work at Branksome Dene has involved closing the beach and of course the beach huts accordingly.'

Not wishing to disappoint her, he even suggested a holiday flat might be the answer.

'Four days to happiness or to put it another way – three days of waiting before I can feel what life and love is really all about. I will try for a beach hut for the day but do not be too disappointed if this should not be and we have to take second best along the beach amongst the motley.'

His sincere words must have given my mother much needed encouragement:

> 'My prayers are really towards the day when I can free you from your present intolerable responsibilities and to offer you a home where you can breathe without disturbing the ire of the other occupants – where you can relax and think of the more pleasurable things in life.'

And in a Christmas card he wrote:

> 'And so, another year has raced by, one that we could ill afford to lose. My main grouse is the comparatively few years remaining. We have not had much time together, but we have got to know and discover things about each other which for my part leave me in no doubt that I chose wisely in having you around me. Your earnestness and devotion have been an inspiration to me particularly in the many moments of concern that have occurred over the past year. Heavens knows what lies in store this coming year, but I know that together we have the kind of love for each other to ride out the crisis and each subsequent crisis as it occurs. God Bless.'

But the loveliest of all the cards was another Christmas greeting:

> 'When God made Lord Jesus
> He gathered ingredients by perfection. Divined for the mortal frame
> For us of course it was different and mother nature became the architect and for you I can well believe she took:
> The Red from the Rose to colour on high,
> The Blue from the Heavens to lighten your eyes,
> The gurgle from the spring to sweeten your voice,
> Honey for your kisses, a master's choice,
> All-in-All, as perfect as can be
> All-in-All my own Honey Bee.'

After reading Howard's letters, I felt happy, sneaky, guilty, but it left me in no doubt that he worshipped my mother.

Their clandestine liaison was yet another chapter in my life that had been cleverly disguised. Although my whole life had revolved around deception and secrets, there was no way I could blame my mother; by furtively conducting her own affair, I am sure she gained gratifying satisfaction.

I felt a glowing contentment knowing she had found love in her life.

CHAPTER 22
THE END IS NIGH

After Connie's move to Southport in 1989, her passion for travelling took on a whole new meaning. For as long as I could recall, she hankered after adventure; surrounded by vast blue oceans from which there was no escape thrilled her. With her addiction to the sea, she made countless excursions on the Geest banana boats to the Caribbean; back then, apart from the cargo, they also took on board a handful of passengers with everyone treated like royalty. A trip on Concorde around the Mediterranean was another of her 'must do' ventures. Cruising on the QE2 gave her the exhilaration she craved, with little time to unpack her suitcase before embarking on the next.

Judging by the comments fellow passengers had written on the covers of the dinner menus, it proved how popular and well-liked she was with everyone she met.

'To the girl who has everything; Great to have met you; You have been great fun; Sincerely hope to see you grace our vessel again soon.'

In Connie's last letter sent from Cape Town in January 2006 she ended it saying:

'I have had a wonderful four months here and Maxine and her husband have really looked after me well. Of course, nobody believes it but I really think it is my last time. As I have told them, I am a liability now. They take me everywhere and my mobility is poor, and they are terrified of me falling so I am being extra careful these next two weeks. I have already had a black eye (self-inflicted), a visit to an eye specialist and a minor eye op and a visit to the doctor for a prescription as the tablets needed aren't available here and another doctor for a blood test as instructed by the Warfarin Clinic back home, so you see what I mean about being a liability. No, sadly, I think it must be, as I said at the onset, my swan song. I have been very lucky to have such wonderful friends here and I have had two excellent places to live...... Lots of love.'

Since my discovery of the role Connie had played during my years of growing up, my visits to Southport had become much less frequent. I questioned why I was still making the tedious trips when all I could do was visualise her in my father's bed, or he in hers, but I had not cut off all communication for the sake of my children; they knew nothing of her sordid past and I was not inclined to disclose to them all the facts. And, of course, I had not yet breathed a word of my findings to Chris. It had become a serious dilemma.

More importantly, I lived in the hope Connie might one day look me in the eye and apologise.

A month after her return from Cape Town saw her admitted into hospital for investigations. She had a slight cough, nothing too troublesome, she told me, but to everyone's concern and against the advice from medical staff, she defiantly discharged herself.

With no definite diagnosis, she became increasingly frustrated and began discussing with me how best to end her life.

'If I can't continue with my holidays,' she said, 'there's no point in hanging around.'

She was adamant that voluntary euthanasia held the answer. It shocked me to think she would contemplate something so drastic. 'It's simple,' she said. Connie had done her homework on Dignitas, the assisted suicide organisation founded in Switzerland in 1998. She appeared relieved that such an establishment existed and with her matter of fact attitude discussed its merits. 'Don't you think it's marvellous that you can end everything with an injection? All that's required is to be sound of judgement.' Just as she had demonstrated all through her life it was her way of wanting to be in control.

Her plans, however, did not eventuate. Illness had crept up on her without warning and, with no further mention of Dignitas, she astounded me when she talked about an overdose. As a young child, her pill popping had always intrigued me; some she took for blood pressure, some were her 'youthful tablets', and with several in the palm of her hand and a flick of her head they would disappear without even a sip of water. 'I've planned my escape when the time beckons,' she told me. 'Suicide kit's to hand. If all fails, my final way out is refusing to eat.' I told her I thought all her suggestions sounded alarming. I could not work the woman out.

As delicate new leaves appeared on the trees in the spring of 2006, Connie's health showed no sign of improvement but her rebellious character remained intact.

Although she had made the decision not to pursue with her ideas to end her life, she'd had another brainwave. And this was her best suggestion yet.

Chris and I had returned from a short break to the New Forest to find a message from Connie on the answerphone. She needed to talk as soon as possible she said. 'I want you to know I've arranged for my body to go for medical research ... to Liverpool University. They'll be sending you the consent form to sign.'

'Medical research?' That's different, I thought. I had heard of people donating their bodies to science, but never dreamt I would be involved in making the necessary arrangements.

'You know I'm not religious, Diane.'

I was aware of that. It seemed of little consequence what happened to her after death.

'And having to go through all the paraphernalia of a funeral is not my thing.'

'It's not as though you'll know anything about it,' I laughed.

'I've decided if I can make just a small contribution to medical science then that's where I wish to go.' She appeared relieved with her decision. 'They keep the body for ... it's something like three years,' making sure I knew what the procedure entailed.

'And when they've finished hacking me about, they'll ring you to discuss what you want to do with me!'

The minute she hung up, I checked out the pros and cons of donating a body to medical science. The person must give consent before death. It was there in black and white. Given that human tissue is potentially dangerous in terms of bacteria and pathogens, the rules are stringent and regulated by the Human Tissue Act. The thought of a student slicing her to pieces on a slab in a laboratory did not bother her in the slightest... and it didn't bother me either.

Connie disliked hospital and did all she could to avoid admittance and on the next occasion when doctors informed her that she would require fluid to be drained from her lungs, she was convinced all the signs pointed to lung cancer, the same disease that had taken my father's life seventeen years earlier.

Once home, she insisted that, with the help of her good neighbours, she would be able to manage. Unfortunately, good as the neighbours were, it came to the point where they were no longer able to cope.

I needed to make urgent arrangements. And that called for Chris and me to thunder up the M6 once more to arrive at the Stafford services by seven for a welcome Americano. At that time of the morning, Costa was quiet and as I sipped my coffee and watched the Little Chef's red security shutters lifting for another day, I contemplated the recent telephone conversation I'd had with Connie's doctor. 'We aren't talking months,' he told me. 'It's weeks.'

His suggestion that she have a fortnight's respite in a care home horrified her.

'Wants what?'

'It'll do you good. He ...'

'Don't care what he recommends.'

I tried to emphasize the benefits. There was no other option. Even Chris was doing his utmost to make her see it would be worthwhile. I wondered whether he would have been so accommodating had he known about her background.

Arrangements happened rapidly and as we pulled into the car park at the rear of the red brick building, I knew what awaited.

'Don't know why you've brought me here,' she said loud enough for all to hear.

'On doctor's orders,' I reminded her.

She had an aversion to the place before we stepped inside.

Light and airy, her room had a pleasant outlook onto the street below. With the necessary forms completed and tea delivered to her room, I was impressed with the reassurance the staff offered. A slight glimmer of hope was a nurse with a South African accent who she related to immediately. She struck up a meaningful conversation and I felt relieved. Connie began reminiscing about her wonderful times in Cape Town. She told her that she was there just after Christmas and having lived her dream over there for eleven years explained that it was a country she had come to identify with and adored. But the second we were on our own her attitude changed.

'This isn't for me,' she announced cradling her head in her hands. 'It's come to something.' Chris flung me an exasperated look.

When we called to see her the following morning my eye was drawn to a vase of dusty plastic flowers on a table in the entrance lobby and, as we signed the register, I was aware of an unpleasant whiff that left me in no doubt where I was visiting.

With a gentle tap on her door we entered. There was no greeting. All Connie could do was criticize the place.

I tried to think of something positive to say but instead let out an elongated breath I didn't know I was holding.

'I *know* this is hell for you, but *please* will you allow yourself to benefit from the rest. Just to help me,' I begged. I was a bloody fool. Why are you doing this, Diane?

'Cannot stay here another day,' Connie said, chewing at her thumb nail. 'I know you don't understand. It's out of the question.' She pleaded like a child.

'For God's sake!' She was the most stubborn person I had ever come across. I wanted to tell her to buck up, but it seemed pointless trying to reason with her. Why couldn't she be like my mother; grateful for every little thing I did for her. But she had always done things on her own terms; that was how she lived her life.

'Listen Diane.' There was no 'Di Di' so I knew she was serious. 'I have to get out of this atrocious place. Today.'

I swore under my breath.

'I'm discharging myself for my own sanity.'

'You can't do that!' I remembered how she had done the same thing when she was in hospital.

'I can. I've got my mobile and I'm ringing Jan to ask her to collect me.'

I was not going to argue. She could do what she pleased.

'I know, Diane, you'll think me morbid.' I knew what was coming. I'd heard it before. 'I just want to die. I've had a good innings. You know I've always said that when I'm a burden to people then that's when it's time to pull the plug.' Her suicide suggestions flashed through my mind. Her broken spirits were there for all to see, just as my mother's had been. She appeared close to crying, but never once had I seen her tears.

By early afternoon Connie had returned home.

But a week later she was back in hospital. Only this time she did not discharge herself. She was weak and fast going downhill.

CHAPTER 23
UNFINISHED BUSINESS

Soon after that frustrating event and with my reluctance cleverly concealed, I was back in my tracks up north, this time to visit Connie in Southport General. Chris felt it our duty to see her, although, for me, I had a hidden agenda. And, as we travelled the M6 listening to the soothing tones of Alex Lester on Radio Two, my confidence brimmed.

Five hours later, hot, and weary we filtered off the motorway at our usual exit. It was ticking towards ten fifteen. 'We'll go straight there,' I ordered, impatient to get this visit over with.

We lapped a congested car park searching for a space but didn't have to wait long before an over-crowded red mini reversed full throttle out of a parking bay.

'Thank God,' Chris said.

'Harding's luck!' I reminded him, a saying from my mother who always marvelled at his fortune whenever he searched for somewhere to park.

'Come on!' I said, slipping my arm through his. He appeared puzzled but unbeknown to him, I was on a mission of a lifetime. That was the moment I felt a deep pang of guilt. It was ludicrous to think I had not yet plucked up the courage to enlighten him about my murky background.

A stifling smell of disinfectant greeted us as we burst through the automatic red sliding doors. I caught sight of a doddery gentleman clutching a laden Tesco carrier and a dad carrying a

223

bunch of yellow chrysanthemums in one arm and a little girl with a card in the other.

It was our first time at this hospital and after checking directions we headed off down a corridor to our right. With our feet striding in sequence, a cleaner acknowledged us with a lethargic lift of her head as we weaved around her bucket and mop.

My body was jittery and my mouth dry.

More intent on reading the overhead signs, Chris endeavoured to keep pace. 'Slow down! It's like you've got a train to catch.'

'Just hurry up!' I urged tugging at his shirt sleeve.

With another rapid turn, I spied the arrow to Ward 4A. I tip-toed the last few yards and stuck my head around the corner. Connie was lying on her bed adjacent to the entrance, her foot dangled limply over the edge of the mattress. The mahogany brown freckle just above her left ankle was visible; a round birthmark the size of a penny that had been the cause of so much fascination as a young child gave me a prickly reminder of just how long I'd known her. I took a sharp intake of breath and wondered if she'd died. But as she lifted her head relief swept over me knowing we had crucial unfinished business.

'Hello dear.' Her voice wavered.

Chris dragged over a couple of grey vinyl chairs alongside her bed, but not before he offered the other two patients one of his encouraging greetings.

'You shouldn't have come all this way. What time d'you leave?'

'Five,' I answered, hoping I hadn't been too hasty with my reply.

'Goodness! I was awake then.' she said, easing herself up on her elbows. I took notice of the gold chain with the antique locket round her neck; I remember years ago she opened it to show me a war-time picture of my father. The implication of it back then was meaningless but now as I studied it, my blood boiled.

The moment was a little stilted.

'Any diagnosis?' I thought I ought to enquire.

'It's my lungs.'

'Oh?'

'I knew all along.' She appeared keen to change the subject.

'Have you brought my paper, Diane, dear? Jan said she'd leave it on the kitchen table for you to bring in.' Jan was one of those rare, hardworking gems who had become a close friend of Connie's, someone she had come to rely on.

Perched on the edge of my seat I explained that we had come straight to the hospital as the road works just before the Manchester ship canal had slowed our journey.

'But hey we're here now!' I tried to appear upbeat. 'Be nearer six when I drop your paper in. Chris wants to run the mower over the lawn.' A slow smile spread across her face.

'Still like to know what's going on in the world,' she said. 'And my crosswords; can't manage without them.'

As we sat making small talk and listened to snippets of news about the other patients, the hour seemed to drag.

'Cup of coffee, luv?' I jumped as an ample-bosomed care assistant gesticulated to the urn. I thanked her but refused; the thought of my lips pressed against a cup some poor soul might have dribbled down made my stomach churn.

With the clatter of the trolley signalling the midday meal it was our cue to retreat.

As we pulled into Connie's tarmac driveway, I gave Chris one of my whatever-are-we-doing-here glances. It irked me to think he wanted to spend time mowing the lawns, but he was adamant.

'It'll be like a meadow if we leave it.'

'You're mad,' I told him. 'Why should we? Let her get a gardener.'

'Why shouldn't I? It's the least I can do.' There seemed little point in arguing, so told myself the sooner we cracked on, the sooner we could make our get-away and the sooner I would get my reward.

The first thing that hit me as I entered the hallway was the unoccupied damp smell of the place and the loud tick of the clock on top of the bureau. As expected, in Connie's absence the post sat heaped on her shaggy crimson carpet; begging letters from animal charities requesting donations, one area where she showed her generosity, and stacks of cards for her eighty-fifth birthday just two days away.

In her Seventies pine kitchen, the one she'd inherited when

she'd moved there after my father's death, were her bits and pieces stacked neatly on her faded yellow Formica table with a note
from Jan requesting us to take them to Connie.

With neglected lawns mowed and borders tended we headed
off to Southport sea front to recharge our batteries. I huddled
close to Chris and pulled up my collar as a chilly wind blew in
from the shore, but we made use of our time with a brisk march
along the promenade. I would have liked to stay longer but was
eager to embark on my final assignment.

By six, there was a choice of spaces in the car park and to my
relief Chris said he would wait in the car.

'Might even shut my eyes before we hit the motorway.'

'Won't be a tick,' I promised. I would not be loitering a moment longer than was necessary. I was relieved to be on my own,
knowing this visit was my last chance to receive what was due to
me.

At that time, the foyer was silent compared to the earlier
madness that resembled a busy arcade. I caught sight of my re-
flection in the swing doors; drawn features with no makeup and
my hair a tousled mess from the gusty conditions. But nothing
mattered, except for one thing.

As my heels click clacked along the deserted corridor it appeared much longer than it did earlier. I burst into the now
familiar ward; this time there was nothing tentative about my entry. I handed over the can't-do-without Times.

'And here's your other bits,' I said, plonking down a Sains-
bury's carrier bag next to a half empty water jug on the bedside
table.

The room was now empty. It was just me and Connie.

Our eyes locked and she thanked me for coming. My adrenalin was pumping at an alarming rate. I knew this visit would be
worthwhile. I was unsure how she was going to explain herself,
but I was here for the listening. I had made up my mind I would
never be the one to broach the subject, it had to come from her.
This was her last chance to offer me an explanation; she must
know there would never be another.

My life flashed before me, as I am sure hers must have done.
Connie may have been wondering what I knew and what I'd
made of it; never once had she spoken about her relationship with

my father and, when my mother died, she said I never talked about her. Surely, she could understand why I would not want to stir up painful memories.

There was a pause that seemed to linger. As if on ceremony I stood next to her bed, as though the floor had put out tentacles and suctioned me to it.

Her hand tried to reach out to mine but I could not allow myself to grasp it. There was no time for sentimental gestures. Her eyes flickered. I thought she was about to drift away.

Without warning she drew a breath. I bit my lip in case it was her last.

'Don't go yet.' It was like a mantra playing over in my head. The hairs on the back of my neck tingled.

She opened her eyes and I sensed they were talking. And then she opened her mouth. She was on the brink of admission. I was convinced.

Like a vice the silence pressed in on me; the only sound was the rapid thud of my heart against my chest.

How was I going to respond? I cleared my throat in anticipation.

I craved to hear the word 'sorry', but felt she owed me so much more. Sorry was not good enough.

But there was nothing. Not a word.

Bitterness rose in my throat as I studied this person in disbelief.

I had built myself up to such a pitch and began to wonder if I had imagined it.

My brief visit had not worked out as I had intended; I had resolved nothing. It seemed I was after something I could never have.

I pounded out of the hospital, ranting, and tutting my way back to the car where Chris was waiting.

'Dear God!' I slammed the door and collapsed into the passenger seat.

'Blimey. Any harder and it'll fall off.'

I wound down my window for fresh air. I had a knot in my chest so tight I thought I might faint.

Diane Harding

CHAPTER 24
A FUNERAL TO ARRANGE

With news of Connie's death all I could think about was her wish to leave her body to medical science and the enormous relief I had lived with knowing a funeral was out of my hands.

But a week later, as I was clearing away the breakfast dishes, the phone rang.

'Mrs Harding?' It was the lady from the Bequeathal Office. We had never met, but I had been expecting a call.

'I'm ringing to tell you that regrettably we will be unable to accept Mrs Berry's body at the teaching hospital.'

'Are you sure?' I steadied myself against the bar stool.

'I'm afraid the Death Certificate states the cause of death is empyema and because carcinoma of the lung has also been identified it does not comply with the rules.' I had never heard of empyema but discovered it's a condition where pus gathers between the lungs and the inner surface of the chest wall. The refusal from the University followed in writing, saying how grateful they were to Connie for her kind and public-spirited gesture in offering to bequeath her body in this way.

'I am just so sorry we could not fulfil her wishes.' That made two of us.

There was no accounting for my disappointment as that meant only one thing. There was a funeral to arrange. And the sooner the better.

'And have you given any thought to the music you would like?' the Minister enquired as we discussed arrangements. There was only one song which summarised her life. *My Way* by Frank Sinatra. He was her idol and he could play her out. And the suggestion that I compile a short speech about my stepmother was out of the question. But I thought of Judy. Knowing she would be out of the country for her auntie Connie's funeral, it seemed fitting that I asked her. She agreed and wrote the following:

> 'Connie grew up with my mother and lifelong friend, Freda Machin, and together from the age of three they lived next door to one another, attending the same schools. Her own mother ran a sweet shop, so she was popular with everybody right from the beginning of her life. I remember her as a glamorous, exciting Auntie. So easy to get along with and chat to. She always showed great interest in people and was always full of encouragement and praise. Connie taught and showed me a lot of good things about life and living. Things which no-one else had done for me. She really was a kind, positive, intelligent, non-judgemental lady. She had a wonderful sense of humour and a refreshingly keen sense of the ridiculous. She taught me to love and care for birds and animals, to love to travel and to keep an open mind, to think the best of people, not to be fearful of what other people thought and to live life to the full and enjoy.'

On 28 July 2006, Chris and I drove up to Southport Crematorium for ten thirty. It was warm and the sun hovered high in a turquoise sky.

In the car park, I spotted a small gathering of local acquaintances Connie had made since settling in Southport. In the remembrance gardens, birds tweeted, and red squirrels scampered amongst the shrubbery and plaques depicting departed ones, as though they had turned out to show their respects to someone who was animal crazy.

Waiting for her to arrive my guilty conscience surfaced as I studied Chris standing solemnly in ignorance.

During the service, prickly shivers raced down my spine and

as I listened to Frank singing his words, he brought me, the child kept in the dark, right into the heart of his meaningful song.

It was a farewell that for me was effortless and I tried to show a degree of composure with a handful of her friends whom I was meeting for the first time.

Thankful it was all over, eight of us made our way to the golf club for a lunchtime wake. This was where Connie had so often dined socially so it seemed a fitting venue and despite Chris doing his utmost to inject a degree of light heartedness into the occasion, there was an uncanny atmosphere that was hard to describe.

I tucked into my topside, willing myself to keep my thoughts under wraps. We nattered, all of us, and made polite conversation around the table until Mavis interrupted the chatter.

'Wasn't Connie a sincere lady. So, kind and, well … thoughtful.'

That did it. My eyes burned into her like lasers. I felt an urge to deliver a posthumous attack; I wanted nothing more than to disclose her destructive nature and secretive life but bit my tongue knowing this was neither the time nor the place. These were her friends, her loyal friends who knew her for what she was, but, at the same time, oblivious of her history.

Lunch over, we said our goodbyes and I thanked everyone for coming. It had been a bizarre day; not one I had given a great deal of thought to beforehand, but the impact of that little service had been mind-blowing. Mentally fatigued, I flopped into the car.

'Think it went well,' Chris said.

'Thank God it's over.'

'Guess we'll be back soon to sort out her ashes,' he continued.

I whipped round in my seat. 'Not if I have my way.'

Chris pulled a quizzical face. 'We discussed her wishes to be buried at sea. You know we did. Because you commented how tidal Southport was when we walked along the pier. Remember?'

I had no intention to involve myself in a conversation about the scattering of ashes. When I had offloaded my secret, he would understand why.

As my mind sprang back and forth into consciousness, we made the best part of our homeward journey in silence until we discovered a diversion from our usual exit off the M5. With our redirection through Bristol I spied a pub called The Hatchet. It pulled me up sharply. I needed to listen to my inner self and bury the hatchet. Only then I would have closure.

But all that would have to wait until I had made one urgent phone call.

CHAPTER 25
DETECTIVE WORK

I needed to contact Maxine. She lives in Cape Town and was Connie's tour guide whenever she visited. It had become a pressing matter. Connie had forewarned me that she had left her a gift of money in her will. Because she had taken her under her wing, I guess it was her way of repaying her gratitude. When I rang to organise the transfer of payment, Maxine appeared delighted to have the opportunity to talk. I listened with interest as she told me that Connie had explained to her how, years ago, she had lived over there with a family.

'Apparently it was for eleven years,' Maxine said.

'Yes. That family was my family. And the little girl was me.' There was silence the other end of the phone. It was obvious that Maxine knew about my being Connie's stepdaughter, but appeared stunned to discover that Connie had not told her that I was that family from years ago.

My talk with Maxine unnerved me. Why hadn't Connie disclosed all the facts and how many others were clueless about her background? I couldn't wait to let Linda know of my discovery. My call was sooner than either of us could have imagined but because she had been a crucial part in the writing of this story I felt I needed to tell her and also fill her in on my staggering conversation with Peggy, a close work colleague of Connie's. After she had died, I made contact to see whether she had confided in her about the role she had played in my family. It sickened me to learn that Connie informed her that my mother had consented to the arrangement and was, as she put it, 'happy to share my father. Can you believe that?'

'Happy with it! The woman must have been hard boiled. I hope you put her straight.'

'I did. I spelt out the facts and how Connie's ruthless scheming had resulted in a complete mental breakdown for my mother.' If that was what Connie was telling everyone, then she was making it look like a sordid arrangement. Peggy continued to tell me that Connie was careful with money, prepared to share their tea and coffee instead of supplying her own and that she was laid back with a wonderful smile and was one for 'being looked after'. That was her in every way: the less she could do, the better.

If Connie had told her colleague such an enormous porky, then how many others had she coerced into believing my mother had agreed with the set up? Did she say it to preserve her reputation? And what had she told her sister, for God's sake? It made me think back to the 'Mr Right' she had referred to when I'd had my chat with her all those years ago when we lived in Saltford and, although puzzled at the time, realize that this person who 'might not always be available' was my father.

After my quick natter with Linda, I thought again about her suggestion that I contact Judy in Southport Although I knew all she had told me would be factually correct, I felt I needed further clarification from anyone else who might have known both Connie and my father. Would they be able to throw any light on their characters? Like me, Judy had known her since she was a little girl. Surely, she would be aware of my stepmother's colourful history.

There was also Maureen, the daughter of Mrs Tansey with whom, after the war, my father had lodged while away on business. Because she had known him since she was a teenager, I hoped she too might be able to give me an insight into his personality.

When Chris reminded me that he would be in the States on business the following week, I jumped at the opportunity, knowing I could quiz these people without him around. The sooner he knew about my dysfunctional upbringing the better but for now I needed to capitalise while he was out of the country.

I emailed Judy and by evening I had heard back to say she would be delighted to meet up. I decided that I would travel to Southport to see her on the Saturday and make my way back down to Worcester during the afternoon in readiness for my visit to Maureen on the Sunday.

After an early rise, it was hard to believe that I was back in my tracks up north.

Judy and I had not seen one another since her auntie Connie had died and it felt reassuring that I was off to discuss my stepmother with someone who had known her for years. Like a detective about to solve a crime, I hoped she would be receptive to my questioning, which of course was my reason for visiting. The scenario played over in my head for much of the week. How would she react? Was I about to offend her by revealing her aunt's past? I had no idea what to expect or what I had let myself in for. I warmed to her the first time I met her: she was instantly likeable so I hoped nothing would change because of our meeting.

The nearer I got to Southport, the more agitated I began to feel. With time to spare, I pulled in a nearby cul-de-sac and to calm the butterflies in my stomach turned on the radio. I thought about Chris and wished he were with me for support.

Before I'd had chance to ring the doorbell, Judy appeared. We hugged and I immediately felt at ease as we discussed the transformation Connie's house opposite had undergone since I was last there. She ushered me into her hallway and explained that her feline companion, Thomas, did not take kindly to visitors, but I was happy to risk a starving tiger to extract what information I could.

I strolled round her cottage garden, admiring her herbaceous borders and heard birds tweeting in the overgrown forsythia, but my mind was elsewhere. Half an hour into my visit and I still had not been able to hint at my reason for sitting next to Judy on the sofa in her front room drinking coffee. It didn't seem right to launch into Connie's background straight away, so instead I listened to her snippets of news about the college where she lectured and the coming and going of various neighbours. I knew how fond she was of her auntie Connie; she spoke highly of her so I hoped she would receive my bombshell kindly and see it from my point of view.

I could have gone straight to the point. So, did you know Connie was my father's mistress? Or were you aware Connie and my father had been involved in an affair that spanned my entire childhood? Or was Judy playing me at my own game; had she sussed why I was visiting and preferred not to be the first to mention her name? There was no knowing what she was thinking, and I only hoped I would have the courage to come out with my questions and not falter at the last minute.

My stomach lurched as I waited for an appropriate gap in the conversation and with that Judy recapped how her mother, Freda, and Connie had grown up together and had won scholarships to the Grammar School in Walsall. She had mentioned her name. I had my opening.

'So, what do you know about Connie's past?' My voice wavered as I asked the crucial question.

'Well, Connie told me how much she loved your father and that she didn't get married until she was fifty-four. My dad always told me how she'd ruined your parents' marriage. That's all I know.' Her voice came over calm and sensitive. 'I was told Auntie Connie foisted herself on the family in South Africa.'

'Oh, yes!' I started my story from the beginning. 'She was my father's mistress.' As the last syllable left my lips I burst into tears. I wiped my eyes with the back of my hand and tried to regain composure. The moment had allowed me to release so many pent-up emotions. Judy wrapped her arm around me, and I apologised for being stupid. 'Her arrival was the end of my childhood as I'd known it.'

'Oh Diane! I never knew the extent of the cover up. I can't believe what I'm hearing.'

'And when Connie was in a coma, I guess people wondered why I hadn't rushed to be at her bedside.'

Judy let me know if that had been her, there was no way she would have travelled to see her during her illness, let alone when she was dying. I felt relieved to hear her say that.

'I admire you for your restraint and dignity,' she told me. It was kind of her to pay me a compliment but that was not what I had come for.

'It's shocking, Diane!' She studied me as I continued to unravel the facts. 'Do you think she was amoral?' It had never crossed my mind, but it seemed a possibility.

'I did wonder whether you knew of her sordid past but it's not something one asks.'

'Well it's obvious Connie carried no guilt and no regrets, and was oblivious to what people thought. You don't think she was emotionally autistic as well, do you?' Judy arched her eyebrows in horror.

'Well that would make sense. She was a dangerous lady and beyond thick skinned.'

'Like I said, Connie told me how much she adored your father and how she loved life and got everything she wanted.'

'She and my father were both as wicked as one another.'

We darted about in conversation and Judy told me that when Connie moved up to Southport to live opposite her parents, after a while, their friendship became strained. It seemed Connie had called on Freda's husband, Sam, to do endless jobs. Freda told her that he was not getting any younger and that she was taking advantage of his DIY skills.

They also disapproved of her endless globe trotting; Judy said she thought they were jealous as they could not afford such luxurious holidays themselves and, it seems, Connie had a reputation of being careful with her money. She said friends wondered whether that was the reason for her extravagant breaks.

'When you were living in Birmingham, I know Connie worked for Cadbury's at their Bournville site.' Judy was trying to put her movements into perspective.

'Really?'

'I don't know where she was living but I know she worked there.'

I'd always wondered where she was while we were in Moseley.

'Not sure how long it was for,' Judy said.

'Until we moved to Surrey, I bet.' I wondered if my father had given her a lift to work every day, just as he had done back in Cape Town. And then I wondered who followed whom? Did we move to Surrey because Connie had found a job at the record shop in London? I'd always thought she'd gone to work there as soon as we arrived back in this country.

That was another missing piece of the puzzle which I had

not picked up on and, as my mind raced back to our time in Moseley, I questioned whether that was the reason my father arrived home late every Friday. Again, my mother must have had her suspicions but never breathed a word.

Connie's deviousness had clearly shocked Judy and I could not help wondering how many others she might have involved in her stories, especially on her cruises after an evening of gin and tonics.

'I'd always known part of it but not the full extent,' Judy admitted. 'It was amoral of her.' She kept repeating it. 'It's obvious she didn't care what people thought. Oh, my goodness, Diane. Poor you! And your poor mother!'

As soon as I was able, I checked the exact meaning of amoral. The dictionary definition said, 'Lacking a moral sense, unconcerned with the rightness and wrongness of something and having no principles or restraints.' That was Connie to a tee. No feelings and no misgivings. I then looked up the definition of emotionally autistic. It said, 'Lacking in facial expression, inflexible to feelings, no gestures to show emotional interaction.' Connie showed no empathy or sensitivity. Again, those traits summed up her character and I could understand why Judy thought she fell into that category. I knew there had to be a reason for her hardened behaviour. That description summed up my father too. I knew now what made him tick. Finally, I had my answer.

I explained how Connie had admitted being an atheist and that she had no desire to have anything to do with the Church; that she didn't believe in its ridiculousness and had no time in her life for God or the Bible, quite the opposite to my mother who relied on Him to help her through her dark days. If Connie had good reason, she never said. Although, she did tell me there was one occasion when she decided to show her face at Church; it was soon after moving up to Southport when a friend had coerced her into giving it a go. She would enjoy it, she told her and benefit from her findings. It surprised me that Connie showed willing and wondered whether she thought she had missed out on something important in her life. But her attendance had the opposite effect; in no way was she ever going near the place again, her visit that day was definite proof that the holy establishment was not for her. Perhaps because of her lack of faith, she had no compunction about wronging God and no worries about any afterlife.

With so much to talk about, I had monopolised the afternoon. I felt indebted to Judy for being so honest and open with me, both of us equally alarmed at what the other had to say.

I did not want to leave on bad terms but when she gave me a bear hug, I felt comforted to know she was on my side.

We parted company and agreed to keep in touch.

Following my fact-finding visit to Southport, I headed off to Worcester and checked in to the quintessential white rendered hotel woven into a steeply wooded copse high in the Malvern Hills, a gem of a resting place Chris and I had discovered quite by accident during one of our previous missions up north.

As the setting sun poured its tangerine glow over the surrounding countryside, I sat in the tranquil gardens and reflected on my time with Judy. I sent her a text to thank her for her hospitality, for her understanding and for listening to me droning on for three hours. I received one back immediately to tell me how lovely it was to meet up and that she was still in shock. She also mentioned that she had spoken to her brother and sister who told her the only person who would have known any in depth details about Connie's reputation would have been their mother, but she never spoke of it. Her motto was the least said the better. I was also intrigued to learn that her aunt would have nothing to do with Connie.

Over a glass of wine with dinner, a charming waitress called Olivia struck up conversation. In a dining room deserted of guests, she appeared relieved to have someone to talk with. She thought she recognised me and asked whether I was a secret celebrity. I played along with her and jokingly told her not yet but that I was on a fact-finding mission for my book. She wanted to know what it was about. I told her it was an intriguing story from my Cape Town days. Again, I retreated into my shell of secrecy. There was no way I was going to give her any inkling of my past. It was still an uncomfortable subject.

I went to bed that night with my head in a whirl. Tomorrow would be Maureen's turn for an interrogation.

I woke at dawn to wild quadraphonic birdsong and immediately felt I was in another world.

Because my meeting wasn't until mid-morning, I set off to

explore the rugged charm of the Malvern Way. A herd of hefty Dexter cows lined the route and a bracing breeze made progress along the escarpment tricky, but, an hour later, I felt refreshed and ready for my reunion.

It was years since the pair of us had seen one another and I was curious to know whether she had aged much. Now in her eighties, I found her just as I had remembered. Wearing a delicate pink jumper that offset her naturally silver hair, she had a pretty face, a high-pitched voice and a warm smile as welcoming as the last time we met. I could see why my father had always remarked on her attractiveness. It was obvious he had always had an eye for the ladies.

I placed my potted cream orchid on Maureen's polished hall stand and could not help noticing how pristine and orderly everything appeared. 'Come on in, dear,' she said, ushering me into a lounge flooded with welcoming sunlight.

The pair of us chatted non-stop and an hour into our conversation I made another intriguing discovery. Maureen screwed up her face in dismay when I confided my background. I listened with interest as she explained that, although she was aware my parents had divorced, and that my father had remarried, and yes, she did know it was Connie as my father had taken her to meet her, she was clueless about the goings on all those years ago in Cape Town.

'I'd no idea Connie was over there living with you all. Goodness, Diane.' It was the same reaction Judy had shown towards me. 'It's so awful. To think your father behaved like that. He was always such a charmer. And so caring. He's gone right down in my estimation.'

And, just as I had with Judy, when Maureen told me what a delightful lady my mother was and how with her strong features and hair swept back in a bun she resembled a ballerina, elegant and with poise, again I embarrassed myself and broke down. If ever my mother came into any conversation and, especially when they sang her praises, I realized my emotions were still just beneath the surface.

One fascinating snippet I heard was how Maureen's mother, Mrs Tansey, had, before the war, mislaid her wedding ring. She bought a cheap replacement from Samuels the jewellers, because, as Maureen explained, with two children it was vital to have a ring on her finger. But she later recovered the missing ring and on one of my father's visits gave him the one she had bought. It left me wondering whether that could have been the wedding ring he in turn gave to my mother on their wedding day as it was during the war when money was scarce. I have that ring in my possession and will be looking at it in a different light.

And when Maureen asked me about my feelings towards Connie I did not hold back.

My search for the truth had sent me on many missions. Wynne, my cousin, was the last person I hoped I could quiz. His father, Billy, my father's younger brother, had settled in South Africa prior to my parents' arrival. I saw little of Wynne and his sister, Anne, as they lived in Rhodesia (now Zimbabwe) as I was growing up, but when the family made a rare visit to our home in Newlands, I remember how my father teased me saying he was going to knit me a string bra. He would often joke about it but in front of my good-looking teenage cousin I felt myself flush with embarrassment.

Had Wynne's parents offloaded any facts about his uncle Vic's past? It would be good to hear his side of the story. I had tried, unsuccessfully, to contact him so I sent a Christmas card with my phone number. My endeavours paid off. I plucked up courage and explained my reason for getting in touch but before I'd posed my question, he told me:

'Connie was Uncle Vic's lover.'

My jaw dropped. 'So, you knew?'

'Oh yees.'

His harsh South African accent took me back. It made me wonder who else was privy to my strange upbringing and why the person most affected was the last to know. It gave me great satisfaction to learn that, after their visit to Newlands, Anne had assumed Connie was the maid and my mother a film star.

Having moved back to this country with his family some years later, he went on to tell me that when they visited us in Sea Mills, he thought Connie was 'open and friendly' whereas he found my mother 'stern and distant'. It came as no surprise that she displayed her irritation.

Diane Harding

CHAPTER 26
CLOSURE AT LAST

Prior to Chris's return from the States, I sent him a text to forewarn him that I had news about Connie, as though it might slip my mind. I figured that by putting it down in print, I would have no excuse to renege on my decision to tell him about my unorthodox homelife.

It had been an anxious wait and I have no idea why but within hours of his homecoming he suggested we collect Connie's ashes from the undertakers.

'Need to get it sorted.'

'Not doing it.'

'You have to.' He gave a disbelieving laugh to think I was not adhering to her wishes.

'Sod it! There's nothing in her will to that effect. Her request to scatter her ashes at sea was merely a verbal one. I'll ring the undertakers and tell them to disperse of them where they think fit.'

And with that, my moment had arrived. I felt I was about to give the performance of a lifetime. My whole body was shaking with first night nerves. I told myself to calm down, knowing just how dangerous it is to get uptight, blood pressure and all that, but I had no control over my emotions. I was anxious how he might react; shamefully, it was something I had put off a thousand times. When everything was out in the open, I hoped he would understand the real reason for my odd behaviour and quick temper whenever he mentioned Connie's name. And he would under-stand my restless nights and constant dreaming. That vivid nightmare when I'd woken up in a cold sweat, fuming at a scenar-io I couldn't explain. Finally, he would be able to appreciate what had been festering for so long.

'Here, sit by me.' I bunched up in the chair to make space. I cleared my throat. 'I've been putting off this evil moment.'

'What's happened since I've been away?'

'I know you're aware that Connie's been in my family for years … from way back. That's what really pissed Mum off. Well I'm ashamed to say, and this is going to floor you … well … Con-nie was my father's mistress during all that time!'

I said it all in a whisper. I was embarrassed for myself and embarrassed for Chris. 'Yes, and before you say anything, I only made the grim discovery that half term when I sorted through Mum's papers. All the evidence was in that box of hers. Ages ago, I know. It's something I've been living with. You can imagine how I've felt.'

Chris made no comment. He stared into space, frozen, as though decoding my every word. 'Well I knew your poor mum was unhappy. The reason she left home.
But …'

'Now perhaps you can understand why I stormed out of the hospital in a rage in Southport. All I wanted was to hear the woman repent. She couldn't even do that. There was no way I could tell you. It's been hard to let go … and … please don't think badly of me. I'm sorry,' I blubbed on his shoulder. 'I've wanted to say something since unearthing the evidence but it's so ugly I couldn't bring myself to do it. But I'd made up my mind today was the day.'

My voice croaked as I explained things from the beginning. 'And … Connie hung on for another eleven years once we were back in this country until she finally managed to become Mrs Ber-ry. Eleven *bloody* years.'

'What a bastard! I was never sure what to make of your fa-ther. He treated your mum with contempt. And he certainly never considered you … all that upheaval of changing schools. I was so worried when you were unwell soon after we got married. It all makes sense now.' Chris grabbed my hands and looked me in the eye. 'Take it from me you've got nothing to be embarrassed about.'

And then he said something along the lines that when he first met Connie, she seemed so genuine but obviously a woman who was scheming. His reaction was understandable, knowing he was completely in the dark, just like me. He knew my mother had loathed her continual presence, but I also knew she was someone he regarded as easy-going and a natural optimist. In fact, he would joke sometimes just how laid back she was. He asked her once how come she never worried. 'What's the point. Only gives you grey hairs,' was her response. And now, suddenly, it had hit home that there was a darker side to her.

'And she couldn't even express regret. To think I'd spent the last three years pining for something it seemed I could never have.'

'Then why didn't you confront her?'

'I was determined that it had to come from her. I didn't feel it my responsibility to demand an explanation.'

'She obviously felt she'd done nothing wrong.'

'How can you say that!'

'For all you know she might have begged your father to leave you and your mum from the start, but he put his foot down. And then you wouldn't have had a father in your life. Perhaps, just like your mother, you were the reason he didn't walk away.'

Chris's comment pulled me up sharply. It had never crossed my mind. If that was a possibility, then perhaps I had featured in his life. I am sure my father did love me – he only ever wanted a daughter – but I could never excuse his evil behaviour.

'It's a classic case of coercive control,' Chris said. 'It would be considered unlawful today.'

'Thanks for being so understanding.'

'Look, there's two ways you can tackle this.' As always Chris tried to inject normality into an awkward situation. 'Connie has obviously tainted your whole life and the hatred has turned to bitterness. But you'll have to think how long you want to harbour these feelings. You don't want to be someone with a massive grudge so you can either hang onto it or choose to bury it.'

Those were profound words. His sympathetic ear jolted me back to my senses.

He was right. I didn't want to be someone with a grudge. No-one would benefit. I would have to let go of my anger and throw the resentment I'd been storing 'over my shoulder' as I would tell my mother whenever she felt wound up. I was determined not to allow my past to spoil my future. It was obvious that Connie was one of those people who would never be able to ask for mercy. Knowing the magnitude of her wrongdoing, I decided that it was not only her egotistical way that had prevented her but that both she and my father had no compunction departing this world without seeking forgiveness.

'That's it! I'm burying that bloody hatchet!' I thought back to the promise I made to myself after we drove past the pub on our way home from Connie's funeral. It was futile to harbour regrets. It was my life. My revelation had affected nobody but me.

My determination to understand my past had taken me on many missions to many places to talk to many people but all those interviews had left me with more questions than answers. But what I know now is that there were two wrongdoers in the relationship. In my mind I had always pointed the finger at Connie, the seductress, but perhaps I had pointed the blame unfairly.

Like a crime, I fear I will never solve the matter regardless how hard I try and whatever theories I come up with. I needed to accept what I knew I could never change. It was time to move on. Offloading my dark secret was like a cleansing process. I felt rejuvenated, as though I had metamorphosed into freedom.

With all bitter thoughts back in that box I would emerge a stronger person, only this time, I would leave them in there securely for evermore, determined to put my energies into my own wonderful family and their present-day demands. And, if I could provide my children with just half the joy and enthusiasm my mother had instilled in me, I knew it would be a job well done.

With Connie's death I now had liberty to write about anyone and anything. And whenever arguments spiralled, those childhood promises I made to my mother that it would one day go down in print carried a far greater determination now that I had unearthed the facts. To put the record straight was the revenge I had been waiting for.

The greatest lesson I have learnt is that to succeed in life you have to experience the tough times.

I have often dreamed of what might have happened had I confronted Connie. How she would have reacted and what she might have said, but of course that could only ever be in my imagination.

That and telling my story will have to suffice.

Diane Harding

Diane celebrating her 60th birthday

ACKNOWLEDGEMENTS

This book is the memory of many, in particular my aunt Linda who provided me with information I was never aware of. My indebted gratitude goes to her and to those who in the early stages of my writing gave me hope; Kevan Manwaring for his Creative Writing courses, Iris Jones Simantel for ploughing through my manuscript on numerous occasions and Kylie Fitzpatrick for steering me towards my goal. Thanks also to my dear friend, Maddie Drury, who enquired tirelessly about the book's progress.

An enormous thank you also goes to my wonderful family and husband, Chris, for his patience and endless encouragement during those long nights of writing.

But none of this would be possible without my brilliant editor, Carol Trow, for her time and valuable feedback and to Nicky and her team at BLKDOG Publishing for their friendly and efficient manner in pulling the book together and making my dream come true.

Other titles by BLKDOG Publishing for your consideration:

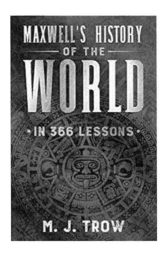

Maxwell's History of the World in 366 Lessons
By M. J. Trow

Peter Maxwell is the History teacher you wish you'd had. If you meet anyone (and you will) who says 'I hate History. It's boring,' they weren't taught by Mad Max.

Many of you will know him as the crime-solving sleuth (along with his police-person wife, Jacquie) in the Maxwell series by M.J. Trow (along with *his* non-policeperson wife, Carol, aka Maryanne Coleman – uncredited!) but what he is *paid* to do is teach History. And to that end has brought – and continues to bring – culture to thousands.

In his 'blog' (Dinosaur Maxwell doesn't really know what that is) written in 2012, the year in which the world was supposed to end, but mysteriously didn't, you will find all sorts of fascinating fac-toids about the *only* important subject on the school curriculum. So, if you weren't lucky enough to be taught by Max, or you've forgotten all the History you ever knew, here is your chance to play catch-up. The 'blog' has been edited by Maxwell's friend, the crime writer M.J. Trow, who writes almost as though he knows what the Great Man was thinking.

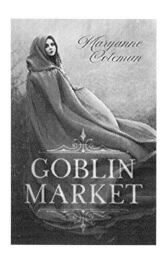

Goblin Market
By Maryanne Coleman

Have you ever wondered what happened to the faeries you used to believe in? They lived at the bottom of the garden and left rings in the grass and sparkling glamour in the air to remind you where they were. But that was then – now you might find them in places you might not think to look. They might be stacking shelves, delivering milk or weighing babies at the clinic. Open your eyes and keep your wits about you and you might see them.

But no one is looking any more and that is hard for a Faerie Queen to bear and Titania has had enough. When Titania stamps her foot, everyone in Faerieland jumps; publicity is what they need. Television, magazines. But that sort of thing is much more the remit of the bad boys of the Unseelie Court, the ones who weave a new kind of magic; the World Wide Web. Here is Puck re-learning how to fly; Leanne the agent who really is a vampire; Oberon's Boys playing cards behind the wainscoting; Black Annis, the bag-lady from Hainault, all gathered in a Restoration comedy that is strictly twenty-first century.

Prester John: Africa's Lost King
By Richard Denham

He sits on his jewelled throne on the Horn of Africa in the maps of the sixteenth century. He can see his whole empire reflected in a mirror outside his palace. He carries three crosses into battle and each cross is guarded by one hundred thousand men. He was with St Thomas in the third century when he set up a Christian church in India. He came like a thunderbolt out of the far East eight centuries later, to rescue the crusaders clinging on to Jerusalem. And he was still there when Portuguese explorers went looking for him in the fifteenth century.

He went by different names. The priest who was also a king was Ong Khan; he was Genghis Khan; he was Lebna Dengel. Above all, he was a Christian king who ruled a vast empire full of magical wonders: men with faces in their chests; men with huge, backward-facing feet; rivers and seas made of sand. His lands lay next to the earthly Paradise which had once been the Garden of Eden. He wrote letters to popes and princes. He promised salvation and hope to generations.

But it was noticeable that as men looked outward, exploring more of the natural world; as science replaced superstition and the age of miracles faded, Prester John was always elsewhere. He was beyond the Mountains of the Moon, at the edge of the earth, near the mouth of Hell.

Was he real? Did he ever exist? This book will take you on a journey of a lifetime, to worlds that might have been, but never were. It will take you, if you are brave enough, into the world of Prester John.

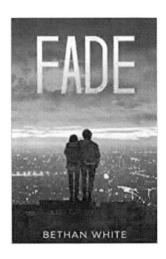

Fade
By Bethan White

There is nothing extraordinary about Chris Rowan. Each day he wakes to the same faces, has the same breakfast, the same commute, the same sort of homes he tries to rent out to unsuspecting tenants.

There is nothing extraordinary about Chris Rowan. That is apart from the black dog that haunts his nightmares and an unexpected encounter with a long forgotten demon from his past. A nudge that will send Chris on his own downward spiral, from which there may be no escape.

There is nothing extraordinary about Chris Rowan...

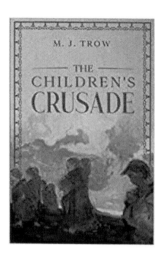

The Children's Crusade
By M. J. Trow

In the summer of 1212, 30,000 children from towns and villages all over France and Germany left their homes and families and began a crusade. Their aim; to retake Jerusalem, the holiest city in the world, for God and for Christ. They carried crosses and they believed, because the Bible told them so, that they could cross the sea like Moses. The walls of Jerusalem would fall, like Jericho's did for Joshua.

It was the age of miracles – anything was possible. Kings ignored the Children; so did popes and bishops. The handful of Church chroniclers who wrote about them were usually disparaging. They were delusional, they were inspired not by God, but the Devil. Their crusade was doomed from the start.

None of them reached Outremer, the Holy Land. They turned back, exhausted. Some fell ill on the way; others died. Others still were probably sold into slavery to the Saracens – the very Muslims who had taken Jerusalem in the first place.

We only know of three of them by name – Stephen, Nicholas and Otto. One of them was a shepherd, another a ploughboy, the third a scholar. The oldest was probably fourteen. Today, in a world where nobody believes in miracles, the Children of 1212 have almost been forgotten.

Almost… but not quite…

The poet Robert Browning caught the mood in his haunting poem, *The Pied Piper of Hamelin*, bringing to later readers the sad image of a lost generation, wandering a road to who knew where.

The Vulture King
By Nikki Turner

Orphaned Aram has survived alone for five years, his only friend a thieving magpie, who acts as his eyes. For in the Carrionlands, magic comes at a terrible price. It costs you your sight, hearing or voice.

When he rescues a voiceless girl, Bina, from being sacrificed to the Vulture King, he is taken in by an underground resistance group. They reveal that Aram's mother is alive, but the king is using her and other slave magicians to fuel his unnaturally long life.

With his mother's magic being rapidly drained, she doesn't have long to live. If Aram can find the Radix, a hidden magical power source, there's a slim chance he might be able to save her. But to get there, he must cross the Barrens where every living creature is out to kill you. That's if one of his new companions doesn't betray him first.

www.blkdogpublishing.com